CATALOG OF HUMAN SOULS
Book 3

I0091227

HUMAN MANIPULATION MODES
Either You Are Manipulating
Or You Are Being Manipulated

Olga Skorbatyuk and Kate Bazilevsky

HPA Press

ISBN-10: 0996731229
ISBN-13: 978-0-9967312-2-5

Olga Skorbatyuk and Kate Bazilevsky
Human Manipulation Modes: Either You Are Manipulating Or You Are Being Manipulated.

Part 3 Chapter 2 translated by Kate Bazilevsky.
All images are in the public domain unless otherwise noted.

© 2015 Olga Skorbatyuk, Kate Bazilevsky
Part 3 Chapter 2 © 2005 Andrey Davydov, Olga Skorbatyuk
© 2015 HPA Press
All rights reserved.

Dedicated to the 40th anniversary of the discovery of the Catalog of Human Population by researcher Andrey Davydov.

Table of Contents

PREFACE

Sketch © 2000 Andrey Davydov

We—authors of the Catalog of Human Souls book series—would like to briefly describe what these books are about right from the beginning because the topic of the Catalog of Human Population is very new for many people.

These books are dedicated to the 40th anniversary from the beginning of research that led to discovery of the Catalog of Human Population. A technology of uncovering of the individual structure of human psyche (or simply put—the soul) was created on the basis of this scientific discovery. The author of scientific discovery of the Catalog of Human Population and this technology is a researcher of ancient books, an expert in Chinese culture Andrey Davydov.

The source of knowledge about the structure of human psyche and the basis for creation of this technology is one of the most ancient and mysterious texts preserved in this civilization—the ancient Chinese monument Shan Hai Jing (translated as the Catalog of Mountains and Seas), which Andrey Davydov managed to decrypt.

After Andrey Davydov created the technology of decryption of Shan Hai Jing (Catalog of Mountains and Seas), it was found that this ancient Chinese monument contains very detailed descriptions of 293 models of human psyche and a lot of other kind of information about the structure of *Homo sapiens*. On this basis, Shan Hai Jing was qualified as the Catalog of Human Population.

In Shan Hai Jing (Catalog Mountains and Seas), the biological type "human" is described as a type divided into 293 subtype structures according to the phenological principle. It turned out that each person, belonging to one of these 293 subtypes from birth, has stable characteristics of this subtype; regardless of race, nationality and particularities of parental psychophysiological structures, which are only minor correctors.

Information about the subtype structure is implanted in the form of a program in the unconscious of a person from birth, and this program determines all of his life: his/her personal qualities and character properties, algorithms of life and functioning, hidden motivational spring, abilities, talents, preferences, inclinations, etc. Natural subtype program is that what is called "psyche", "soul."

Natural program is that individuality, which makes a person different from other people as representatives of other subtype structures of biological type *Homo sapiens*. Each individual "speaks his own language," specified by his subtype program, as the language of values, views, convictions, preferences, which are standard and unchanging for all representatives of a subtype.

In the language of science, a natural subtype program of *Homo sapiens* is called Individual Archetypal Pattern; in simple language—an Individual (Subtype) Program, an Individual Program or a Program.

A human program is recorded in the language of natural images. Images or, using the language of science, archetypes of the unconscious sphere of a person is the language of human "software." The concept of "an archetype" was introduced to psychology by Carl Gustav Jung, but as it turned out, archetypes can be not only of the collective unconscious, but also individual. Therefore, to avoid confusion, in popular texts we prefer to call the language of "software" of *Homo sapiens* by the word "image" instead of "archetype."

Programs of each of 293 human subtypes are recorded by different natural images and a different number of images, meaning that they are endemic, are not similar to one another. *Homo sapiens* is a living system, which, as it turned out, exists and functions strictly on the basis of a natural program implanted from birth, and from this it was concluded that a human is a bio-robot at the genetic level.

The conclusion that "*Homo sapiens* is a bio-robot" is confirmed by that learning someone's natural individual (subtype) program from the Catalog of Mountains and Seas as the Catalog of Human Population, it is possible to find out absolutely everything about this person in great detail; about any aspect of his life and activities, including that what he or she carefully conceals.

In addition, *Homo sapiens*, as a biosystem programmed by nature, has modes of self-regulation and regulation (control from the outside). Modes of regulation are a natural inborn mechanism, just like an individual human program. Their discoverer Andrey Davydov named these modes Individual Manipulation Modes (Manipulation Modes for short). This management tool, which can be applied to any person, also was found in the text of the ancient Chinese monument Shan Hai Jing.

It was found that for every person, as a biosystem, there are three manipulation modes: suppressing, balancing and stimulating. Manipulation modes together with an individual (subtype) program are individual structure of psyche of *Homo sapiens*. Programs and manipulation modes of each subtype differ, from one another. For this reason, people differ from each other by internal characteristics, and individual manipulation scenarios are necessary for each person.

Structure Of Psyche Of *Homo Sapiens*

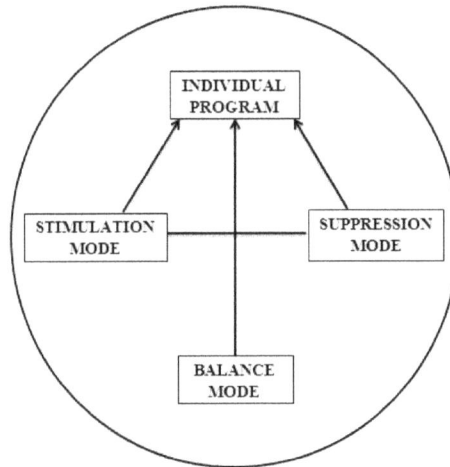

© 2015 Olga Skorbatyuk, Kate Bazilevsky

Individual program, with which a person was born, is the main segment of structure of human psyche (soul). Knowing the natural individual program allows you to find out who he/she (or you personally) is real, without masks, what motives drive this person (or you), and so on.

Suppression mode is a self-control mode, which turns on automatically as a mode of relaxation, pleasure, dream, happy oblivion (a "turn off" button). It is the individual program of people, who belong to a particular subtype. When a manipulator acts out a personality from the suppression mode, it makes an individual experience pleasure, unconsciously get attached to the manipulator (fall in love, etc.), and on this basis obey him/her and fulfill all of his/her requests/demands.

Balance mode is a self-control mode, which turns on automatically when a person needs to become balanced, get in a harmonious, comfortable state without loss of activeness. It is the individual program of people, who belong to a particular subtype. When a manipulator acts out a personality from the balance mode, it makes an individual experience comfort in communication with him/her, trust him/her at the unconscious level and consider him/her the best friend.

Stimulation mode is a self-control mode, which turns on automatically when a person needs to stimulate himself/herself to some actions, become active. It is the individual program of people, who belong to a particular subtype. When a manipulator transmits properties of the stimulation mode in a certain way, it makes an individual experience strong irritation, up to wild rage, and on this basis he/she does that what a manipulator asks for/demands.

Natural manipulation modes described in Shan Hai Jing (Catalog of Mountains and Seas) as the Catalog of Human Population provide a key to managing any person. With the help of knowledge of human manipulation modes, it is possible to factually change a person's physical and psychological state, behavior, reactions in the desired direction.

No one is able to resist application of his personal manipulation modes because it is a natural mechanism, which is built into human psyche from birth. Therefore, information about manipulation modes of a subtype provides unlimited possibilities for influencing any individual as a representative of this subtype and allows self-control and control of any human as a biosystem.

Non-traditional psychoanalysis, a new direction in scientific psychology, allows identifying an individual's subtype structure (psyche) and manipulation modes on the basis of the Catalog of Human Population. It is called non-traditional because it does not use any of the traditional principles, approaches to the study of human psyche, as well as methods (observation, experiment, testing, biographical method, questioning, conversation) since these methods are not needed in order to obtain any kind of information about a person as a stable and identifiable biosystem.

A non-traditional psychoanalyst knows what a person is like, what problems might concern him or her and why, and how these problems can be effectively solved without any kind of contact with this person. All that a non-traditional psychoanalyst needs to know about the subject being studied is the day, the month, the year of his or her birth and the gender. Neither race nor nationality or place of residence of the person being studied matter because the Catalog of Human Population contains descriptions of unchanging characteristics of subtypes of *Homo sapiens* of the entire human population.

For colleagues from the scientific environment we are offering our definition of what human psyche and the Catalog of Human Population are: "*The Catalog of Human Population is a description of a human as a type by subtype structures. Subtype structure ("psyche", "soul") is a combination of individual archetypes, recorded at the genetic level (principle). Expressions and interaction of subtype structures in manipulation modes and phenological algorithms are described with adjustments for gender, age and cultural differences. Information is recorded on six factors.*" This definition was developed by Andrey Davydov—the author of discovery and decryption of the Catalog of Human Population.

It is also necessary to tell a bit about the main source of knowledge (knowledge of that *Homo sapiens* are bio-robots, that human psyche (soul) is "software," that "software" of any person can be easily uncovered, and so on), which was obtained in the course of our scientific research. To date, no one knows for sure who gave and preserved this knowledge, but after it was written down it got the title 山海經 Shan Hai Jing (translated from Chinese as Canon/Catalog of Mountains and Seas).

According to Artem I. Kobzev (a Russian historian of Chinese philosophy, Doctor of Philosophical Sciences, professor, author of over eight hundred scientific papers on the history of Chinese philosophy, science and culture), Shan Hai Jing is an anonymous monument, which presumably dates back to the late III century BC-early II century BC. It consists of eighteen juan (scrolls), combined into two sections: Canon/Book of the Mountains (Shan Jing) or Canon of Five Innermost Mountains (Wu Zang Jing) in five juan and Canon of the Seas (Hai Jing) in thirteen juan.

Legend claims that Shan Hai Jing was engraved on sacred vessels by Bo Yi—an assistant to the wise semi-mythical ruler of the ancient times Yu the Great, who lived in the XXIII century BC. Yu the Great entered the throne in 2205 BC. Authors of the Han epoch attribute authorship of the literary monument Shan Hai Jing to Yu the Great and his companion Bo Yi.

According to legend, Yu the Great dealt with a great flood, which fell upon earth and arranged it. The deedful ruler allegedly came to know its mountains, rivers, their spirits, as well as animals and plants. He ordered his assistant to describe everything that was seen. As a result, these recordings together with images of spirits, fantastic animals, birds and plants were engraved on nine ritual vessels-tripods. Later on, these sacred vessels were lost. However, according to historical annals, prior to their strange disappearance, the text of the Catalog of Mountains and Seas, along with amazing images of representatives of flora and fauna, spirits and deities were copied.

This answers the question why some date Shan Hai Jing back to III-II centuries BC, while others back to XXIII century BC—the Catalog of Mountains and Seas as the source of information appeared during the time of Yu the Great and it got the form of a text much later. We tend to agree with those researchers, who date Shan Hai Jing back to XXIII BC since according to Dan Zhu the Catalog of Mountains and Sea was recorded only after its long-term oral existence (this point of view is expressed in his commentaries to the famous monument Spring and Autumn - Chunqiu). Reports that Yu the Great and his assistant Bo Yi created the Catalog of Mountains and Seas exist in, for example, Wang Chong's (27-97 AD) treatise titled Critical Essays: "When Yu and Bo Yi were taming the waters of the flood—Yu was engaged in calming the water, while Bo Yi in recording information about various "things." And, they created the Catalog of Mountains and Seas."

We will add that apparently in mythologies of almost all cultures of the world (those, which to continue to exist, as well as those, which already sank into oblivion) exist facts, which show that the Catalog of Human Population was present in these cultures. This is not difficult to trace by carefully studying the ancient, archaic cultural layers. However, the source itself was preserved only in one culture—the culture of China. This is not surprising since Chinese culture is not only ancient, but also, in spite of everything, the Chinese manage to preserve it and their traditions from the ancient times to the present day (unlike representatives of other cultures).

This was a brief description of the main points, about which you will be able to learn in detail from the Catalog of Human Souls book series.

*****

In essence, the Catalog of Human Souls book series is one book divided into five parts. All these parts are devoted to a single topic—scientific discovery made by researcher Andrey Davydov, the Catalog of Human Population. Division into five parts was done because materials for this book are quite non-uniform in content and style.

The book Catalog of Human Souls is divided into five parts since fundamental research being carried out by Andrey Davydov and our colleagues is interdisciplinary, and the field of research is wide and multifaceted (psychology, gender relations, sociology, political science, linguistics, sinology and so on), and also because we present results of this research not only in the language of science, but also in the language of popular science.

In addition, we (authors of Catalog of Human Souls books), who are presenting research and discoveries of our laboratory's research supervisor Andrey Davydov, found it necessary to include some information about him as well. It seemed to us that the story of discovery of the Catalog of Human Population might be of interest not only to those, who are already familiar with it, but also to those, who are just learning about the Catalog.

Also, in order not to sound groundless, we decided to offer readers to get acquainted with some of materials from the Catalog of Human Population. These materials are provided in the form of brief demonstration versions from descriptions of natural programs of people. We are of the opinion that presentation of any, even the most captivating scientific theory is, as the saying goes, not worth even a straw, if this theory cannot be tested and used on practice.

Demos that we presented certainly are very short and they are by no means complete descriptions of individuals. However, perhaps they will be quite enough for independent testing, which even a non-professional in the field of psychology will be able to do and get a confirmation that the Catalog of Human Souls (a nonscientific title of the Catalog of Human Population) really exists. And, this means that now he or she can use this Catalog in daily life.

We—authors of the Catalog of Human Souls book series—have the honor to not only tell about some of the research done by our laboratory's research supervisor Andrey Davydov and our colleagues, but also to participate in the development of the Catalog of Human Population. However, it must be stated right away that in all sections where we tell about the technology, methodology of non-traditional psychoanalysis—we are only narrators. Technology of decryption of the ancient Chinese monument Shan Hai Jing was created over 20 years ago and its authorship belongs to Andrey Davydov.

*****

The Catalog of Human Souls book series contains the following five books:

Book 1. *Homo Sapiens* Are Bio-Robots. Human "Software" (by Olga Skorbatyuk and Kate Bazilevsky). This book tells about the new method of obtaining information from the unconscious sphere of a human and about the Catalog of Human Population in the form of answers to the most frequently asked questions. In this book, we also presented three hundred selected research topics, which were developed in our laboratory between 1974 and 2014.

Book 2. Hack Anyone's Soul. 100 Demos Of Human Programs From The Catalog Of Human Population (by Olga Skorbatyuk and Kate Bazilevsky). In this book, we are offering one hundred brief demonstration versions taken from descriptions of human programs in the Catalog of Human Population. Of course, these descriptions are only a tiny fraction of information that the Catalog contains about each person.

However, we think that this is enough for independent testing and to obtain confirmation of existence of the Catalog of Human Population.

Book 3. Human Manipulation Modes. Either You Are Manipulating Or You Are Being Manipulated (by Olga Skorbatyuk and Kate Bazilevsky). This book is entirely devoted to manipulation modes—the natural toolkit for controlling a system called "a human," which was discovered in the ancient Chinese monument Shan Hai Jing (which turned out to be the Catalog of Human Population). In this book, we explain what individual manipulation modes are and how to use them to manipulate people. After all, with the discovery of the Catalog of Human Population, only two positions in society are left—either you are manipulating or you are being manipulated. And, as proof of that this is really so, in this book we provided the scenario of suppression mode for manipulation of people, who were born on October 12th of leap years or October 13th of common years. Despite that this is only one of four modes of manipulation of those people, who were born on the dates indicated—it will be sufficient for testing.

Book 4. Non-Traditional Psychoanalysis. Selected Scientific Articles And Presentations at Conferences (by Andrey Davydov and Olga Skorbatyuk). This book presents some of the scientific articles and presentations at scientific conferences done by Andrey Davydov, the author of scientific discovery of the Catalog of Human Population. It also includes several scientific articles (which are also chapters of the textbook titled Archetypal Pattern. Fundamentals of Non-Traditional Psychoanalysis.), authors of which are founders of non-traditional psychoanalysis: Andrey Davydov and his colleague—psychologist Olga Skorbatyuk.

Book 5. Shan Hai Jing—A Book Covered With Blood. The Story Of Developers of the Catalog of Human Population (by Kate Bazilevsky). This book uncovers the story of developers of the Catalog of Human Population—Andrey Davydov and Olga Skorbatyuk— that is related to obtaining of political asylum in the United States of America due to many years of persecution by the Federal Security Service of Russian Federation (FSB, former KGB) and attempts to kill them in order to take possession of their research product—the Catalog of Human Population.

*****

From the beginning, as authors of the book series Catalog of Human Souls, we would like to apologize for the lack of a single language style and popular language. Our colleagues from the scientific environment, professional psychologists or those, who are interested in scientific psychology, can satisfy their curiosity about the theory that lies at the basis of technology that we use to identify the individual structure of psyche in

Book 4 of this series (Non-Traditional Psychoanalysis. Selected Scientific Articles And Presentations At Conferences.).

The other four books in this series are intended for the widest audience. From our point of view, any person, regardless of education level, must have an opportunity to get acquainted with results of our research. After all, Shan Hai Jing, as the Catalog of Human Population, was left to all humanity. Therefore, in many of our books (despite that they are all devoted exclusively to scientific topics) we try to use the literary language, avoiding frequent use of specific terminology. However, we were unable not to use jargon at all, and for this we beg your pardon. We are not writers, our main work is scientific research, and in books we are sharing with the audience some of the results of this activity, according to the common practice in the scientific community.

Speaking of language that we use to describe the topic of our research... It was noticed that some people are perplexed by that we use the word "soul," as it is not customary to use this word in the scientific community. However, as it was found, human soul, which is the same as psyche and subtype structure—exists. And, it exists regardless of someone's opinions about it.

Soul (psyche), as "software" of *Homo sapiens* is not a psychological, religious or metaphysical value—as it turned out, it is purely a natural value. Therefore, like any natural phenomenon (rain, wind, electricity, gravity), the soul functions regardless of whether people know about it or not, and regardless of what they think about this. People can argue as much as they want whether soul exists or not, and fantasize as much as they want about what it is, but the natural mechanism called "soul" will continue to work. In every person, while he is alive.

Therefore, every person has the right to continue debating whether or not the soul exists and fantasize about what it is, but we prefer to study the human soul as an existing phenomenon (which, by the way, is possible to see, hear, smell and touch, if you have information about individual structures of psyche) and use results of this research on practice.

We consider the question of what words to use to call the natural phenomenon "soul" unimportant when it is possible to study it as a phenomenon instead of talking about it. We use the word "soul" because in any language it accurately reflects the essence of the phenomenon—that foundation, on the basis of which any human being lives, and because of which he is alive; that what is called "closer than the body." And, unlike our colleagues-psychologists, we are not forgetting that "psychology" translated from the ancient Greek means "science about the soul" (from the ancient Greek ψυχή - "soul," λόγος - "teaching").

*****

Now, let's get back to the Catalog of Human Souls books series. Those people, who are already familiar with our research and our other books, usually have questions, to some of which we would like to provide answers in the Catalog of Human Souls book series. For example, people are interested to know who exactly is working on compiling of the Catalog of Human Population, and why it is not possible to find information anywhere, including on the Internet, about all members of our laboratory's staff. Also, people want to know how they can get information from the Catalog of Human Population about themselves or other people.

With regard to the question about developers of the Catalog of Human Population and other staff members of our laboratory, it really is difficult to find reliable information about them and here is why. This happens for two reasons: the first reason is explained using an example with the Internet in the Introduction to Book 1 of this series titled Homo sapiens Are Bio-Robots, and the second reason is confidentiality of all of this kind of information and is related to security. The number people in our laboratory, who work on compiling of the Catalog of Human Population, is not three people, as it might seem. However, unfortunately, we cannot provide any information about who these people are. Reasons for this are detailed in Book 5 of this series (Shan Hai Jing—A Book Covered With Blood. The Story Of Developers Of The Catalog Of Human Population).

Due to persecution because of the main subject of our scientific research—the Catalog of Human Population—by a group of employees of Federal Security Service of Russian Federation (FSB, former KGB), headed by colonel of Foreign Intelligence Service (data for the period 2000-2004) Andrey Dmitrievich Polonchuk, we do not have the right to provide any kind of information about our laboratory's staff. You can get acquainted with the evidence of these prosecutions in Book 5 mentioned above. Originals of documents presented there are stored in the United States Department of Homeland Security, Federal Bureau of Investigation (FBI), etc.

Therefore, if anywhere in public sources, for example on the Internet, you come across a statement that someone is an employee of the Special Scientific Info-Analytical Laboratory—Catalog Of Human Souls or the Human Population Academy, and is engaged in developments related to decryption of Shan Hai Jing and compilation of the Catalog of Human Population—it can be either disinformation or fraud, or both. However, we do have partners and affiliates. Therefore, it is always best to check with us.

Beware that some research works of Andrey Davydov (the author of discovery of the Catalog of Human Population) and the Special Scientific Info-Analytical Laboratory—Catalog Of Human Souls led by him were stolen by a group of employees of the Federal Security Service of Russia (formerly KGB) headed by Andrey Dmitrievich Polonchuk—colonel of SVR FSB of Russian Federation (information about his rank refers to 2000-2004). Therefore, it is possible to find offers on the Internet (in different languages) to purchase information from the Catalog of Human Population, even though this information is in no way related to the Catalog or to natural human "software."

Such offers can be found at the following websites: in Russian – Mountains and Seas of Self-Knowledge http://mountaseas.com, Catalog of Human Population (Catalog of Mountains and Seas) http://vk.com/chp_lab, Find The Answer Within Yourself http://www.facebook.com/groups/mountaseas.2905/, Catalog of Human Population http://vk.com/googlite; in English – Shan Hai Jing Lab/Shan Hai Jing Laboratory http://www.facebook.com/SHJLab/info, http://twitter.com/SHJLab and http://shjlab.wordpress.com; etc.

It is extremely dangerous to buy products offered by fraudsters. Since some time back Andrey Davydov suspected that sooner or later, in one form or another piracy will occur and made some inaccuracies in materials related to Shan Hai Jing; without taking them into account it is impossible to correctly put together the base material.

Perhaps, after realizing this A. D. Polonchuk's group decided to get at least some, at least material benefits from stolen works and this is how a strange, ugly product was born, which has nothing to do with information from the Catalog of Human Population as the decrypted ancient Chinese monument Shan Hai Jing.

The consequence of this is that those, who get information from fraudsters cause irreparable damage to their health; both physical and psychical. Unfortunately, our laboratory already has a significant amount of information about cases when people, who requested information from the Catalog of Human Population from those, who officially have nothing to do with this research, experienced serious damage in various matters and of varying degree of severity. The reason for this is the fact that human psychophysiology functions on the basis of images. Therefore, if a person receives images and decryptions (which essentially are images as well), which are in no way related to his/her personal psychophysiology and begins to use this information on practice, then consequences might be as follows:

- psychical disorders of any kind, which cannot be cured

- somatic disorders of any kind, which cannot be cured

- death, as a result of psychical and physiological disorders

Therefore, please be careful. You have every right to turn to anyone for information from the Catalog, but we issued this warning and we will not be held responsible in any way for possible consequences of your decisions.

You can get information from the Catalog of Human Population about yourself or any other person directly from our laboratory right now. For convenience of our clients, the system of issuance of any kind of information directly from developers of the Catalog of Human Population is made in such a way that they do not need to contact us. Anyone can view prices and pay for an order here - https://www.humanpopulationacademy.org/pricing/.

And, for those people, who would like to not just get materials from the Catalog of Human Population sold on our website, but also contact us (for example, with a business proposal, to order of some specific services, to get consultations, to become a student, etc.)—please refer to Human Population Academy's Contacts page at https://www.humanpopulationacademy.org/breakthrough-discovery/contacts/.

Purchasing information from the Catalog through our website or by contacting us are the only ways to get information from the Catalog of Human Population directly from its developer without the risk of coming across fraudsters.

It should be noted that no one ever persecuted our clients; they never were and are not in any danger because those who persecuted and continue to persecute us were never interested in our clients as they do not have information about the technology of decryption of Shan Hai Jing. In addition, we always respect confidentiality of any person, who turns to us for information from the Catalog and we never share information about our clients with anyone.

*****

In conclusion, we would like to state the principled position that we adhere to as authors of books (and, currently there are over three hundred of them)—we do not in any way claim to be gurus; we are more comfortable with the position of students. However, due to the fact that we engaged and continue to engage in research work, we are able to obtain information that can be interesting and useful not only to us. And, we are just legalizing this information for those, who prefer not to believe, but to know. To know how the world works and what is his or her own, personal structure.

Another principal point is that in our books, we do not share our personal opinions, hypotheses. Everything that we state is information from the ancient sources that we are studying and facts obtained during the course of our research activities, which have been tested, as it is customary in scientific practice. We prefer to keep to ourselves our opinions and fantasies, as insignificant in comparison with that what is stated in our books.

Also, on behalf of our colleagues from the laboratory and ourselves, in celebration of the 40th anniversary since the beginning of research of the ancient Chinese monument Shan Hai Jing as the Catalog of Human Population, we would like to express deep gratitude to all of our relatives, friends, acquaintances and colleagues from the scientific environment, as well as to all others, whom we happened to come across in life, for that they failed to prevent us from carrying out this research.

Olga Skorbatyuk and Kate Bazilevsky
Los Angeles, California
June 2015

INTRODUCTION

NOW YOU ARE EITHER A MANIPULATOR OR YOU ARE A SUBJECT FOR MANIPULATION

Sketch © 2000 Andrey Davydov

People instantly bristle and express their indignation when manipulation is being discussed. However, in his soul every person dreams of finally finding a method that allows influencing others with one hundred percent guarantee. And, preferably, imperceptibly in order to continue to manipulate "thy neighbor," while declaring that "manipulation is unethical, immoral, disgusting" and "I never manipulate anyone." Your dreams came true—such a tool was found.

However, do not rejoice too much. There are two more pieces of news you. According to a well-known joke, one is bad and the other—very bad. The first one is that this tool has nothing in common with "super-psychotechnologies" that you are being threatened by on every corner, but influence of which only make you come do a reasonable conclusion: "It is impossible to manipulate me." Now people will manipulate you and they will be successful at it. And, it is very likely that this is already being done to you since the second piece of news is that this tool is already (and has been for a long time) in use by the public.

This tool is called natural manipulation modes. They are correction modes of psychophysiological state and behavior of a person. Manipulation modes are a purely natural mechanism. Using technological terms, they are the "factory settings" of Mother Nature itself; they are built into the structure of psyche of *Homo sapiens* at the level of instincts and unconditioned reflexes—meaning, inborn reactions of an organism to certain influences of the external or the internal environment. Therefore, no human being can resist the application of his/her own manipulation modes.

Manipulation modes are implanted in the unconscious part of human psyche since birth. Any representative of the biological type *Homo sapiens* has three of these modes: suppressing, balancing and stimulating. Originally, they are modes of self-correction and self-regulation intended to ensure that a human could regulate the state of his psychophysiology and behavior from within himself. However, as it turned out, if you know natural manipulation modes of an individual, and transmit them towards him/her from the outside, then he/she becomes one hundred percent controllable like a robot-machine.

It is a priori impossible to notice the influence of application of natural manipulation modes of a human. The influence bypasses consciousness and intellect of the subject of manipulation. No one is able to notice transmittance of natural manipulation modes towards him/her, regardless of his/her professional skills, educational level, life experience and intuition, as these modes are an inherent part of individual structure of human psyche. They are his/her own, native; what is called—"closer than skin."

Probably, the unprecedented power of this tool and its effectiveness are due to that it is a nature's creation. Nobody invented or developed manipulation modes. Information about this natural mechanism and practical tool for managing a human are of a very archaic origin. Both were accidentally found by a Russian researcher-sinologist Andrey Davydov, while he was studying one very ancient source. The title of this source is 山海經 Shan Hai Jing (translated from Chinese as the Catalog of Mountains and Seas).

Authorship and the exact dating of Shan Hai Jing are still unknown. However, according to some experts, it dates back to XXIII century BC. The existence of this book has long been known. The ancient Chinese philosopher Confucius (IV-V centuries BC) was familiar with it, but prior to the discovery made by Andrey Davydov no one even supposed what kind of information is encrypted in this ancient source. However, despite that the researcher was able to uncover the secret of Shan Hai Jing and find out that this ancient Chinese monument is nothing other than the original "instruction to *Homo sapiens*," the description of a blueprint, pattern of human psyche—this source still remains mysterious. At least because it is still unknown who left the writings with this knowledge to people.

We think that it is easy to conclude from everything stated above that your favorite mantra "It is impossible to manipulate me" will no longer help you. Despite that your fantasies about being unmanageable will remain with you and just like before you will feel absolute freedom, independence and randomness of all of your actions—if someone will want you to, then you will twitch like a puppet on invisible strings. All that now remains in your power it to decide whether to continue being a subject for someone's manipulations or to choose the position of a manipulator. There is no third option anymore.

*****

As Andrey Davydov found in the course of research, each person has his own "control buttons," and partly for this reason all known methods of psychophysiological influence work on one person, but not on another. For this reason, the natural mechanism that he discovered was named "individual manipulation modes."

It is also possible to influence *Homo sapiens* using common and artificially created schemes because all people are representatives of the same biological type. However, artificial schemes will never make a human one hundred percent manageable. And, it is possible to gain control over the entire psychophysiology of an individual without weakening his health and ability to work, which is important for the "puppet masters." However, for this they need to know that what modern psychologists and other "soul-experts" do not know: how *Homo sapiens* is arranged in terms of natural psychical apparatus, what psyche is in general, what its structure is and on what bases it works.

Answers to all these questions were obtained by Andrey Davydov and his colleagues in research during the course of many years of studying 山海經 Shan Hai Jing and other ancient texts. In Shan Hai Jing, in addition to about one thousand descriptions of natural manipulation modes of *Homo sapiens*, Andrey Davydov found detailed descriptions of two hundred and ninety three models of structure of human psyche (or, using the simple language, soul). However, the soul does not mean a mysterious and amorphous philosophical-religious concept, but rather a natural phenomenon, which works like software for computers.

As it turned out, the soul is not some unknowable fleshless essence that exists separately from the body, but rather it is, using the computer terms, a "hard disk" with a program, on the basis of which a person lives and functions, including at the physiological level. The only thing about which the mystics and adepts of religions were right is that the soul is the basis, the foundation of existence of an individual. However, before Andrey Davydov no one considered the soul as a magnitude that can be known in the tiniest details, and not by the means of esoteric or religious revelations, but exclusively by scientific methods.

Soul (or psyche, whatever you prefer to call it) is nothing other than a natural biological program. If we continue the analogy with computers, this program gets "installed" by nature. Its work begins at the moment when a human being gets separated from the mother's body by the means of cutting of the umbilical cord. From this moment a human begins to live, act and manifest himself solely on the basis of this program; even if he does not know anything about the existence of this program. Moreover, from birth and until death no one is able to go beyond the limits of his/her natural program. From this it was concluded that *Homo sapiens* is the same bio-robot as all other natural objects on planet Earth.

A human exists and functions strictly on the basis of programs, and this is what makes him absolutely knowable and, potentially, completely manageable. Detailed descriptions of natural programs and manipulation modes of *Homo sapiens* are that what 山海經 Shan Hai Jing concealed in itself for thousands of years and on this basis this ancient book was qualified as the Catalog of Human Population.

However, we will not provide details about the scientific discovery of the Catalog of Human Population made by Andrey Davydov. This topic is covered in other books of the Catalog of Human Souls series: *Homo Sapiens Is A Bio-Robot*, *Hacked Souls*, and *Non-Traditional Psychoanalysis*. Here, we will just say that human "software" is now identifiable using the decryption technology for Shan Hai Jing that was created by Andrey Davydov. Over twenty years of experimental base with discrepancy criterion of less than three percent (which in psychology is not even considered a discrepancy) confirmed that this technology works.

*****

Despite that for already over twenty years this technology is actively being used in people's daily lives, the fact that the Catalog of Human Population was discovered is as if hidden under a "Cap of Invisibility" from the masses to this day. You will not hear about this scientific discovery on the television or the radio, you will not find a single word about it in newspapers and magazines. Several programs dedicated to the Catalog aired on Russian television in 2005-2006, but that does not count. It certainly is possible to find some information about Shan Hai Jing as the ancient source of knowledge about a human and his psyche on the Internet, but the Internet is turned into a dump, this dump gets filled-up quickly, and any information instantly drowns in the ocean of unimaginable garbage.

Therefore, it is not worth it to search for detailed information about the Catalog of Human Population, its developers and people who use this Catalog anywhere on the Internet except for the official website of the Laboratory and the Academy (http://www.humanpopulationacademy.org), as most likely you will not find anything besides disinformation. There are reasons for this and they are described in the Introduction to the first book in the Catalog of Human Souls series titled *Homo Sapiens* Are Bio-Robots. Human "Software" and in book five titled Shan Hai Jing—A Book Covered With Blood. The Story Of Developers Of The Catalog Of Human Population. Therefore, we will not discuss this in this book. Here we will continue telling about the tool that makes any representative of *Homo sapiens* absolutely controllable. People do not talk about this tool—they simply use it, quietly and without warning.

Moreover, people from different social strata use this tool, not just so-called "makers of destinies" like it was before. However, none of those people, who use the Catalog of Human Population to "hack" someone's psyche ever tell about this to anyone; even to relatives and friends. And, soon you will understand the reason. Therefore, if you feel that something is wrong in your life, if you feel a strong dependence on anyone, if all the time you do that what not you, but someone else needs, then it is highly probable that this "someone" knows your individual natural manipulation modes and uses this knowledge against you.

And, possibly, he/she has been doing it for a long time. Since this technology is being used in practice since the 90s of the XX century; and, not only in Russia. Therefore, on the one hand, so far out of over seven billion people living on planet Earth relatively few know about the Catalog of Human Population, but on the other hand, you have no guarantee that someone, who is familiar with this technology, does not live near you and is not applying it to you personally.

Management of a human using his personal natural manipulation modes occurs absolutely imperceptibly. Therefore, any person with whom you come in contact can manipulate you in this way; even during a brief meeting or in business relations. It is so easy to do that even a child is capable of using this technology, if he is old enough and knows how to read. A manipulator can turn out to be someone you would never suspect since you are sure that you know this person very well or even have control over him/her.

It is impossible to hide from this kind of influence in any way. After all, in order to manipulate soul and body of a human using his personal natural manipulation modes it is not at all necessary to communicate with him tête-a-tête. One can transmit manipulation modes to a person by communicating through social networks, chats, email correspondence, telephone conversations, and even text messages. Even if you never leave your house and do not communicate with anyone this will not protect you from application of your individual manipulation modes.

Money will no longer protect from invasion of the "holy of holies" of a human, meaning his soul and through it—his body. Before money allowed to have at least some security, for example, by hiring bodyguards, getting walled up in a castle or "laying low" in a personal submarine. However, now it is possible to do anything with physiology of any person (as well as to destroy him) without using violent methods.

High social status will not protect against this either. At least because in life of a person of any social level there is always someone with whom he is in contact. Without contacts any human goes mad and dies; this fact has been known for a long time. However, even if we assume that an individual does not communicate with anyone, there are still ways to influence him using knowledge of his individual manipulation modes. However, let's not get into the details.

*****

Information about individual manipulation modes of any one of over seven billion people living on planet Earth is now readily available. First of all, now this information is available without any restrictions. Secondly, in order to get the tool to manage someone only minimal information about that person is needed: his/her date of birth. However, right away we must disappoint astrology fans since connection with the date of birth of a person is not due to influence of planets and stars—it has to do with natural phenological cycles. Those people, who are not familiar with science called "phenology" and want to learn more about this, we recommend reading the Introduction to the second book (Hack Anyone's Soul. 100 Demos Of Human Programs From The Catalog Of Human Population) titled Why It Is Not Worth It To Confuse The Catalog Of Human Population With A Horoscope.

In order to get the tool to control any person you are interested in, all that is necessary to know is the day, month and year of his/her birth. It is necessary to know the year of birth only in order to find out whether it is a leap year or a common year since the Catalog of Human Population is neither astrology, nor numerology. This information can be obtained either directly from the subject you are going to manipulate or, so that you do not cause suspicion, you can easily find it in public records, profiles on social networks, personal documents of a person, forms, etc.

To manipulate another person it is no longer necessary to have special knowledge and skills, be a professional psychologist, a hereditary magician or a representative of the special services, and there is no need to have access to "secret knowledge," classified information, special scientific research, specialized libraries, compromising materials, etc. Information on what exactly needs to be done in order to manipulate any person is now available in a format that is understandable by any person—in the form of manipulation scenarios. These scenarios, describe in detail what to do and how to behave with a person you need to influence. Even a poorly educated person is capable of understanding such scenario; it is enough to simply know how to read.

After reading a scenario, all you need to do is to act out a role, which is described there in detail. And, it is not necessary to be a professional actor in order to do this. Any person is capable of playing a role from a manipulation scenario. People in this civilization are taught to lie, wear masks and play roles since childhood. This is taught not only by the means of words, but also by personal example, which gets assimilated much more effectively. A person is forced to play roles every day, throughout the active part of the day. Therefore, this is nothing new for you and all of you are great at it. Your failures to manipulate other people occur only because you do not know what role to act out towards each specific individual. And, the Catalog of Human Population solves this problem.

In the past a person who wanted, so to speak, to play with another's soul for his own benefit had to know where and how to get information from the Catalog of Human Population. Now this is no longer a problem. Firstly, you can contact us to get information about yourself or someone else from the Catalog. Secondly, some of information from the Catalog has already been published on the Internet. For example:

- ❖ a series of 218 books in Russian *Katalog Chelovecheskikh Dush: Programmnoye Obespecheniye Dushi Muzhchin/Zhenshchin, Rodivshikhsya <Data>* [Catalog of Human Souls: Software of Soul of Men/Women Born On <Date>] (by A. Davydov and O. Skorbatyuk)
- ❖ a series of 39 books in Russian *Katalog Chelovecheskikh Dush: Kak Podchinit' Muzhchin/Zhenshchin, Rozhdonnykh <Data>. Zhenskiy/Muzhskoy Manipulyativnyy Ctsenariy.* [Catalog of

Human Souls: How To Subdue Men/Women Born On <Date>. Female/Male Manipulation Scenario.] (by A. Davydov and O. Skorbatyuk)

❖ a series of 10 books in English *How To Seduce Men/Women Born On <date> Or Secret Sexual Desires of 10 Million People: Demo from Shan Hai Jing Research Discoveries by A. Davydov & O. Skorbatyuk* (by Kate Bazilevsky)

❖ a book in English *How To Seduce Men & Women Born On March 5 Or Secret Sexual Desires of 20 Million People: Demo from Shan Hai Jing research discoveries by A. Davydov & O. Skorbatyuk* (by Kate Bazilevsky)

❖ a book in English *Secret Sexual Desires Of 100 Million People: Seduction Recipes for Men and Women: Demos from Shan Hai Jing Research Discoveries by A. Davydov & O. Skorbatyuk* (by Kate Bazilevsky)

Going forward we plan to continue publishing information on the Internet about individual natural programs and manipulation modes from the Catalog of Human Population of people about whom there are no books yet. We also plan to translate them into other languages. Therefore, if today you did not find books about yourself or about people who interest you—do not worry, as they will appear tomorrow. And, those who do not want to wait can contact us. We described how to do this in the Preface and at the end of each book in this series. We have information about any person you are interested in.

Why are we legalizing this information? Because we know that it is needed by everyone and always. And because we have nothing to hide. Also because we want to restore justice by equalizing odds of all people, so that each person would have the opportunity to choose whether he wants to continue to be a subject for someone's manipulations and to be used or he is more comfortable with a position of a manipulator.

*****

People in this civilization love to fool one another by stating that they have a very negative attitude towards manipulations and that they never engage in anything like it. It is a good story for toddlers, but not for adults, and especially not for those people, who know how human psyche works.

It is an absolutely obvious fact that we all live in a society of manipulators. And, this is quite natural, as very few people in this civilization live like Robinson (the character from a novel by Daniel Defoe)—alone on a desert island. A human lives in a society of his own kind and is always in close interrelations with other people. And, each person constantly needs something from another person; for example, to ensure that a person behaves in a particular way and not in any other, to ensure that a person has a certain attitude towards him, to have a person do something for him (or instead of him), etc. In order to get all of the above, it is necessary to manipulate the other person. A different method does not exist in nature.

People try to come to an agreement with one another in the manner of "We're friends, so let's agree that I will not manipulate you and you will not manipulate me" are not only endlessly naïve, but also are absolutely futile. People are unable not to manipulate each other because manipulation is a part of their natural arrangement; even when it comes to individuals, who are commonly called self-dependent and self-sufficient. And, so-called "friendship" and other types of close relationships provide the maximum number of opportunities to manipulate each other and there is not a single person who does not use this. Those who have a different take on this simply engage in deception and self-deception.

Manipulation of others is not someone's whim, and certainly not someone's evil will. This is how nature arranged it since control modes are built into each *Homo sapiens* from birth. Probably this is arranged in such way so that people could communicate with each other effectively. After all, natural manipulation modes are the language spoken by psychophysiology of an individual, as a representative of one of two hundred and ninety three subtypes of biological type *Homo sapiens*. And, each subtype has its own language.

Natural "software" of an individual is the only language that he understands. The situation with the language in which human soul "speaks" is analogous to the situation with foreign languages—one person cannot understand another person, if he does not know his language. Being part of the soul, meaning—psyche of *Homo sapiens*, manipulation modes are such a powerful tool of influence because it is the only language that the entire psychophysiology of an individual understands; and, understands without words.

The fact that we live in a society built on manipulation as a principle is fully confirmed on practice. Another matter is that people try to manipulate each other by using such primitive methods that it is a pity that they waste an immeasurable amount of time and effort on this. Probably, this is where the notion that "manipulation is bad" came from. Of course, it is bad when you are trying to manipulate someone and he or she notices it, and then you begin to have problems with this person. It is bad when another person is simply does not listen to you, and it is even worse when he listens, but does not hear. It is bad when the other person not only does not want to understand you, but also is incapable of doing it even if he really wanted to.

It is bad when you need something very important from another person, but he does not want to understand this. It is bad when the other person does not see, hear, feel, notice you at all. It is bad when you are trying to get through to another person without any success.

Everything mentioned above is the only reason of total loneliness, one of the serious problems for a human in this civilization. However, this problem is artificial, as there is no loneliness in nature and cannot be. The root cause of this problem is in that people do not have the Catalog of Human Population. After all, in order to communicate with another person and to influence him it is necessary to know him as a specific system. It is necessary to least study the instruction to a person. After all, without instructions it is difficult to use even a home theater system.

However, now "the instruction to a human" is found. Therefore, if before it was possible to hope that attempts to influence you will not be successful— now such hopes are at least naïve. Over twenty years of practice of providing information about manipulation modes from the Catalog of Human Population showed that it is not characteristic of people to think even for a second about whether they should manipulate someone or not when there is a tool that allows to do this effectively and completely unnoticeably. Not even for a second! And, together with this it is still possible to declare anything, including "I never manipulate anyone."

Based on everything stated above it is easy to conclude that those people, who do not know anything about the discovery of the Catalog of Human Population and the existence of natural manipulation modes of *Homo sapiens* are currently in an initially losing position in relation to those, who have this information. Moreover, they are in danger. After all, anyone who wants to and knows their birth dates can influence their entire psychophysiology, their life support systems. Not always with good intentions, but always successfully.

*****

In conclusion we would like to say that we are not suggesting to anyone to believe in what we are telling. We are not apologists of another religion that requires faith. We are engaged in science, and in science it is common to verify any facts on practice. Therefore, in the second book of the Catalog of Human Souls series titled Hack Anyone's Soul. 100 Demos Of Human Programs From The Catalog Of Human Population we provided one hundred demo versions, as very short excerpts from descriptions of natural individual programs of *Homo sapiens* from the Catalog of Human Population so that every person could check himself, on his own experience and confirm that this Catalog really exists. And, in this book we provided a description of one of the natural manipulation modes of people who were born on October 12th of leap years or October 13th of common years.

Despite that by nature each person has not one, but three manipulation modes we think that this will be enough for testing. Since we are offering to test the effect of the suppressing mode of people who were born on October 12th of leap years or October 13th of common years, and this mode turns on in *Homo sapiens* reactions of affection towards the manipulator and mechanisms of subordination to the manipulator. And, there are more than enough test subjects because not only Joe and Mary, whom you know personally were born on October 12th of leap years or October 13th of common years. The population of our planet is over seven billion people and there are two hundred and ninety three human subtypes in nature, and therefore over twenty million people are suitable for this test.

We think that it will not be difficult to see reactions of a subject of manipulation. If you act out the role from the provided scenario for people who were born on October 12th of leap years or October 13th of common years and will do it without arrangements, misrepresentations, additions, inclusion of your personal qualities (which during manipulation should be, so to speak, "put on hold"), then reactions of a subject of manipulation will be clearly visible.

We invite our readers to test this information also because not everyone will be able to get a review or a recommendation for our research product from someone. As mentioned above, people carefully hide the fact that they use the Catalog of Human Population, and this is understandable. For this reason, you will have to accept the fact that you will need to check how the natural tool for controlling a human works on your own. We are contributing to this as much as we can by providing information for testing in this book absolutely for free.

And, if you will want to get the remaining two modes of control of people who were born on October 12th of leap years or October 13th of common years or will want to try out and use the tool to manage people who were born on other dates, then no one is stopping you from contacting us. We have all kinds of information about any person who interests you.

At this point, we bid farewell to those of our readers, who imagine themselves great manipulators and are sure of that they already know everything there is to know in this world. Each person has the right to live in his illusions. It is enough for us that you will not be able to blame the developers of the Catalog of Human Population for that you were not told about the Catalog and about that you can easily be controlled by the use of manipulation modes from this Catalog. Only you yourselves are responsible for consequences of your decisions.

To those people, who prefer to build their lives on a more rational basis than their own fantasies, we invite to continue reading and not only learn from the following chapters of this book about what mechanisms make a person one hundred percent controllable, but also test this on practice. However, before you move on to practical actions it is necessary to at least briefly "dive deeper" into the topic called "natural individual manipulation modes of *Homo sapiens*," and this will be done in the following parts of this book.

PART 1

INDIVIDUAL NATURAL MANIPULATION MODES OF *HOMO SAPIENS* ARE A "LOCK-PICK" FOR "SOUL HACKERS"

Sketch © 2000 Andrey Davydov

CHAPTER 1

MANIPULATION AS A NATURAL PROCESS.
MANIPULATION ETHICS.

If you need to drive somewhere, you get into your car and perform a number of simple steps: insert a key into the ignition, turn it, shift the transmission to "D," and smoothly step on the gas pedal. These actions are called manipulations. If instead of carrying out actions to manipulate a car you tell it something like "Please, start moving!"—then, you will not reach your destination in it. Everything is the same with controlling a human.

Manipulation modes from the Catalog of Human Population, which will be discussed in this book, cannot be bad or good. They are simply a tool. They are natural correctors of state of psychophysiology and behavior of *Homo sapiens*. A human is born with this built-in control mechanism, and therefore manipulation using this tool cannot be immoral, unethical, as it is an ordinary, normal, natural process. And, this process makes any representative of *Homo sapiens* into an obedient automatic machine.

Manipulation, as one person influencing another in order to achieve his personal goals, is usually considered in terms of social processes and social norms. There are still attempts to consider manipulation of a human through the prism of concepts such as "ethics" and "morality." However, manipulation modes of *Homo sapiens*, which were found by researcher-sinologist Andrey Davydov in the ancient Chinese monument Shan Hai

Jing, are a purely natural mechanism. This mechanism is built into the human psyche at the level of instincts and unconditioned reflexes[1]. In this connection, before going into details about the natural manipulation modes, we think that it makes sense to tell about manipulation as a natural process.

*****

We apologize for another excursus to the world of flora and fauna for an example; what to do if humanity has long cataloged animals, but either forgot or did not have time to catalog itself. So, for example, you have an aquarium with goldfish, a dog and a canary, you feed them all as it is necessary, according to science and it does not cross your mind to feed millet to a dog, meat to a canary, fruit to fish. Of course, this might occur, but most likely only in one case—when all animals appear the same and tend to multiply before your uncomprehending gaze.

Seriously speaking, without the Catalog of Human Population the question "What to feed to who?" is unsolvable in principle. Besides, people assume that there is nothing to think about here since "we are all people, we are all humans," and so that what I like and that what suits me must be suitable for and be liked by any other *Homo sapiens*. As a result, figuratively speaking, a canary offers millet to a dog and then is surprised that the dog is not at all interested in this offering. While you are studying another person and trying to guess what he needs, you miss a chance to establish contact with him and, most importantly, to get that what you need from him because the relationship either failed to develop or is already hopelessly ruined.

Turning to psychologists with the question "How to manipulate others?" does not help in solving this problem. Since most manipulation techniques offered by psychologists lead to results described in a well-known joke: "You shook my hand for six minutes, you said my name nineteen times, you tried to repeat all of my gestures, I even picked my nose to confirm this, and now I think you are going to try selling something to me." The only conclusion that can be made with such a manipulation toolkit is that "manipulation is awful."

It is a different matter when a person, who decided to manipulate someone, has an "encyclopedia of *Homo sapiens*," which he can open up and read about any person with whom he/she is in contact or is only going to contact. Since you can win over a cat by giving it some fish or sour cream and a dog by giving it a bone, but cannot get on the right side of a person like this—the "encyclopedia of humans" provides detailed, complete information on how to win over anyone. This is much easier and more convenient, as it seems to us. However, the main thing is that today this is possible due to a discovery made by a Russian researcher Andrey Davydov, who discovered the Catalog of Human Population in the ancient Chinese monument Shan Hai Jing.

You can get information from this Catalog about any person you are interested in just as easily and fully as you learn about any animal (including how to interact with it) from an encyclopedia of animals. All two hundred and ninety three human subtypes are described in this Catalog in great detail. Hence, a question: with such a variety of psychical structures within the biological type *Homo sapiens*, how can a manipulation toolkit consist of just ten, twenty or even, for example, fifty manipulation techniques? After all, representatives of each one of two hundred and ninety three *Homo sapiens* subtypes categorically differ from each other; they all have different natural needs, lifestyles, preferences, goals and objectives. Maybe this lies behind failures in manipulation and very popular opinions such as "manipulation is terrible" and "I don't want to manipulate anyone?"

*****

If we briefly describe the main natural principle of manipulation without going into details, then it has long been known to everyone: give a person what he needs and in return he will give you what you need. However, the problem is that psychologists are not aware of that biological type "human" is divided into two hundred and ninety three subtypes, and they do not know specific psychophysiological needs of representatives of each one of these subtypes. Without having this information, psychology offers nothing besides methods from the category "one for all" or a very limited number of different variants of manipulation developed on an unclear basis. Moreover, it is recommended to use these methods in a "hit and miss fashion"—maybe one of them will work, and that in itself is a colossal waste of manipulator's time and energy.

As it turned out, in nature it is arranged in a different way. A human (*Homo sapiens*) is a bioform (bio-robot) with a program, on the basis of which he functions in space and time, analogous to animal bioforms (bio-robots). And, a human is susceptible to operator's influence in respect to himself (unlike an animal) and external influence. This influence on a person is done by using individual manipulation modes.

In other words, from birth every person belongs to one of two hundred and ninety three subtypes, lives and functions according to his subtype program and has his own, individual manipulation modes. These modes are categorically different from manipulation modes of other subtypes. One can incline a person to carry out any actions and can put him in any psychophysiological state by applying that person's manipulation modes.

Knowing the natural program of a person and his natural manipulation modes, you automatically find out for what he is ready to, so to speak, "sell his motherland." And, this is exactly what you offer to him in exchange for what you need. Everything is very simple. However, without knowing, figuratively speaking, who is a dog, who is a goldfish or who is a canary—it is impossible to accurately determine what a particular person needs. You will not succeed in training and making perform necessary actions even a dog if you offer it food of canaries or goldfish as encouragement.

Therefore, when discussing manipulation as such, by manipulation we do not mean primitive methods that psychologists teach (and, by the way, use themselves, as they simply do not have another toolkit). By manipulation we mean artificially created schemes, application of which put a subject of manipulation in subordinate, parity, leading positions. And, in combinations they cause actions that a subject of manipulation considers necessary, but which were already prognosticated by a manipulator.

*****

As it was already mentioned in the Introduction, by nature each *Homo sapiens* has three manipulation modes: "suppressing", "balancing" and "stimulating." When these modes are applied from the inside, a person regulates the state of his psychophysiology and his behavior. If these same modes get transmitted towards him from the environment, then this turns him into a one hundred percent automatic machine and he fully obeys the will of a manipulator. In this sense psychologists are right in that manipulation is a psychological influence that causes a predetermined response in a person in spite of his will; the only thing is that they cannot offer a working tool without having information from the Catalog of Human Population.

Also, in psychology manipulation was never considered something natural, normal. While in nature there are unions, for example, between plants and fungi, in which each side supplies each other with necessary nutrients without mutual damage. There are similar beneficial interrelations among animals; for example, between crocodiles and birds-"teeth cleaners," between hippopotamuses and birds-cleaners, which eat parasites off of skins of these giants, etc. Something similar can be observed among humans. In our scientific research developments, analogous unions correspond to the "balancing mode."

If we again turn to natural analogues, it is possible to notice that the Russian saying "A pike lives in the lake to keep all fish awake!" and similar sayings in other cultures more fully reflect the nature of the "suppression mode" in human relationships. As for the "stimulating mode," then, for example, scavengers-hyenas always "graze" nearby a pride of lions and they constantly provoke lions to leave the prey so that they could take advantage of it. This makes lions "nervous," but not to an extent to allow hyenas to treat them without respect. And, if impudent hyenas violate the boundaries, then the end is always the same—a hyena gets destroyed by a lion. In our scientific research developments, relationships that are similar to these to some degree correspond to "stimulating mode."

However, in order to fully understand everything stated above, we think that it is necessary to tell about how each of the three natural manipulation modes influence the subject of manipulation. This will be done in the next chapter. However, from our point of view, first it makes sense for every person, who intends to use natural manipulation modes of *Homo sapiens* on practice, to close the question with ethics of manipulation for themselves. Moreover, this problem is thought-up. The only question is: what methods you are using to manipulate another person and with what goals.

*****

Right away we want to mention that we are not going to consider manipulation of a human from the perspective of socially accepted moral and ethical norms. At least because in this civilization, as it turned out, there is no authentic information about what "ethics", "morality" or "good" and "evil" are. Since concepts of morality and ethics should be based on a clear understanding of good and evil, we think that it is useless and pointless to consider public perceptions of ethics.

In terms of natural principles described in the Shan Hai Jing and other ancient sources of knowledge, good means any actions aimed at achievement of psychophysiological well-being of an individual, which contribute to his achievement of the status of a "human." Moreover, under well-being is meant not that what a person who does good considers well-being, but that what well-being is in terms of the natural program of the recipient. In this connection, it is not possible to discuss good, ethics, morality in a civilization without the Catalog of Human Population. All this is simply not there. Hence, there seems no escaping the conclusion that approaching practical application of natural manipulation modes of a human with civilizational measures is inadequate, unreasonable.

In terms of nature, use of manipulation modes of a person in order to establish contact with him is not something from the category of evil in any way. Since these modes are part of natural "software" of *Homo sapiens*[2], for him they are exactly the same food as food for the stomach. A manipulator, who knows manipulation modes of a person and uses them with him in order to get something for himself, thus does a good thing for a person—he "feeds" his entire psychophysiology. Hence (in contrast to traditional manipulation methods) a sense of sympathy for the manipulator (at times even genuine love and adoration) arises in everyone to whom this method of manipulation gets applied. (Since these feelings are always the consequence of application of the suppression mode, and a serious manipulator never operates without this mode.) Hence, he is also willing to do something good, kind for the manipulator, to give him that what he needs. This is normal, natural and note that this does not involve deceit and lies.

That is all about ethics of manipulation. We will just add that in contrast to traditional methods of manipulative influences that people in this civilization use with each other, and which often break and crush psychophysiology of both from the inside, manipulation using natural manipulation modes of *Homo sapiens* from the Catalog of Human Population does not cause any psychophysiological damage to both the subject of manipulation and the manipulator. Of course, if the manipulator does not have the goal to drive the subject manipulation "into a coffin."

However, this is a matter of conscience, decency of separate individuals rather than properties of the natural mechanism called "manipulation modes." Manipulation modes by themselves were created by nature so that people could establish full contact with each other. Like a knife, manipulation modes in themselves are neither good nor bad, they are simply a tool. It is just that some people use a knife to kill and to harm, some use it for cooking, while others, like surgeons, use it as a scalpel to save lives.

In any case, natural manipulation modes, as over twenty years of practice have shown, are the only alternative to violence. And, we think that everyone, who will use this manipulation tool in their daily life, should know about this.

[1] An instinct is a set of inborn tendencies and aspirations expressed in the form of complex automatic behavior. Unconditioned reflexes are permanent inborn reactions of an organism to certain influences from the outside world, are carried out by the nervous system and do not require special conditions for their occurrence.

[2] For those, who are not yet familiar with first, second and fourth books in the Catalog of Human Souls series: natural "software" of *Homo sapiens* consists of four parts: his/her individual program and three manipulation modes (suppressing, balancing, stimulating).

CHAPTER 2

WHAT ARE NATURAL MANIPULATION MODES OF *HOMO SAPIENS* AND WHAT INFLUENCE DOES EACH ONE HAVE ON A HUMAN

As already mentioned, by nature *Homo sapiens* has three manipulation modes: **suppressing, balancing, stimulating**. Despite that separately and in combinations with each other all these modes, in essence, are for correction and self-correction of behavior and psychophysiological states of a person—each one of them influences him in different ways. In this chapter, we will briefly discuss this influence.

However, before going into details about the influence of each of individual manipulation modes on human psyche, the following should be noted. This book will not provide details about human manipulation modes as self-correction modes (self-regulation, self-management), despite that natural manipulation modes are primarily a mechanism for self-regulation.

Yes, without a doubt, *Homo sapiens* engages in self-management daily and quite intensively in order to regulate his internal psychophysiological processes and make the work of his psychophysiology fit in with demands of the environment. And, this is a very important matter, but this book is not about self-control—it is about controlling. A separate book must be devoted to the matter of application of natural manipulation modes for self-manipulation. Therefore, in the following chapters of this book we consider manipulation modes only from the point of view of managing (controlling), and not any other.

*****

The **suppressing mode** got its title because with the application of this mode one person begins to obey another. Moreover, he does not notice this at all. And, he does this with great pleasure. Suppression (obedience) occurs when a person onto whom this mode is projected feels like a being, who happily submits to a manipulator as to a deity.

Considering a manipulator as a deity, a subject of manipulation feels a wide range of emotions for him: from sympathy and respect to deepest admiration. In communication with a manipulator, a subject of manipulation experiences a strong sense of pleasure, which prevents resistance to attempts of subordination. As a result, figuratively speaking, a person toward whom his personal **suppressing mode** is transmitted[1]— automatically gets put in a position of a rabbit before a boa. This comparison most fully reflects the nature of the **suppressing mode** in human relations.

A person toward whom his **suppressing mode** gets transmitted obeys a manipulator for one reason only—he feels incredibly well, pleasant, he is happy and we will tell about this in great detail in the next part of this book. A subject of manipulation is ready to do that what a manipulator needs with only one purpose: to be able to continue to receive such wonderful, such pleasant sensations. There is simply no other reason.

The second natural manipulation mode of *Homo sapiens* called **balancing mode** is the mode of balancing, harmonizing human psychophysiology. It represents those qualities and characteristics of another individual, which put a person in a state of comfort and balance; hence, the title of this mode.

A person onto whom this mode is projected feels very comfortable. And, the one who transmits qualities of his **balancing mode** (a manipulator) to him, a subject of manipulation considers his best friend, with whom he feels at ease and has complete mutual understanding, and who like no one else understands his aspirations and needs. Hence, he trusts a manipulator (this trust arises unconsciously), who might not have friendly objectives in relation to a subject of manipulation.

During transmissions of qualities and properties of the natural **stimulating mode**, a person being influenced feels irritation, rejection, resentment in the range from very mild to severe, literally infuriating. A subject of manipulation feels only what is called negativity towards a person (or people), who have qualities of this mode (not necessarily a manipulator).

In small doses **stimulating mode** can effectively and quickly bring a person to certain constructive actions, and in large doses it can cause a severe outbreak of aggression and destructive actions toward someone else (and himself). If a manipulator uses this mode skillfully, carefully and correctly, then in this sense he is not in danger. However, if a manipulator does not know how to transmit this mode toward a subject of manipulation or just by a coincidence demonstrates qualities and algorithms of his natural **stimulating mode**, then he receives all the negativity personally. And, playing around with this is not recommended.

While on the topic of the stimulating mode of a human, we can add the following. Those who use neuro-linguistic programming (NLP) with application of the famous "method of mirroring" are risking rather greatly. Since the entire psychophysiological functioning of any *Homo sapiens*—bio-robot day after day occurs based on a very simple scheme: a person as if flows from one part of his natural "software" into another. As already mentioned, there are four such parts: individual program of a person and his/her three manipulation modes. Therefore, a manipulator, who uses the method of "mirroring" due to lack of knowledge of natural manipulation modes of a subject of manipulation risks "mirroring" manifestations of his stimulating mode, which occur in the mode of self-regulation. Then, instead of getting on the right side of a subject of manipulation, a manipulator will cause strongest irritation, rejection and negative attitude toward himself together with all the consequences. For this reason, in previous chapters we stated that from our point of view all methods of human control that exist in psychology and do not take into account his "software" are surprisingly primitive or, to put it less mildly, stupid.

*****

We will briefly describe how each one of the three manipulation modes—**suppressing, balancing, stimulating**—influences a person when applied from the outside (by another person or people).

The **suppression mode** of *Homo sapiens* is the mode of his subjugation. However, above all, the **suppression mode** is the mode of incredible pleasure. Transmissions of the natural **suppression mode** towards the subject of manipulation put him in a state of euphoria that will outdo the effect from use of any drug.

Immediately after the start of transmissions of the **suppression mode** towards a person, he/she "gets hooked" like a drug addict, and consequently begins to require "a dose" of pleasure from his/her

suppression mode again and again. And, he/she is no longer able to stop.

The **suppressing manipulation mode** is also a mode of a cherished dream. Everything that a particular person dreams about is nothing other than the content of his/her natural **suppression mode**; by nature a human—bio-robot cannot desire anything of his own (anything that he thought-up). Specifically for this reason the subject of manipulation has no chance to disobey the manipulator, who, in essence, offers the embodiment of the cherished dream; and not just one dream, but often all of them at once.

During transmission of the **suppression mode**, analysis of the situation and the personality of the manipulator is absolutely impossible for the subject of manipulation. The **suppression mode** completely disorients a person in a situation and circumstances, and makes him/her obey the manipulator "automatically."

A pleasant benefit from manipulations when using the **suppression mode** is that the subject of manipulation not only falls in love with the manipulator, but literally begins to adore him/her. Specifically on this basis, the subject of manipulation is ready to fulfill any requests/demands of the manipulator. And, in contrast to all other methods of manipulation, he does this with pleasure.

The **balance mode** puts the subject of manipulation in a very comfortable, but at the same time in a very non-critical state. Transmissions of the **balancing mode** force the recipient to regard the manipulator as a friend, while, very likely, he is not.

The comfortable state, which the manipulator causes in the subject of manipulation by transmitting his natural **balancing mode**, automatically makes him trust the manipulator, while this trust is absolutely unconscious and is not based on anything. As the saying goes, "the door of the soul opens up."

The **stimulation mode** makes the subject of manipulation experience such a powerful irritation that he begins not only, figuratively speaking, "to run on the wall," but also on the ceiling. From application of his natural **stimulating mode** the subject of manipulation becomes mentally deranged from anger and is ready to do anything in order to stop transmittance of this mode towards him.

Stimulation mode turns the subject of manipulation into a kamikaze, who is ready to make any actions, which the manipulator needs. With the help of this mode it is possible to make any person do anything. Even that what he/she would never do voluntarily, and that what will possibly cause him/her irreparable harm or that what he/she will regret for a long time.

At the same time (and this also applies to the other two manipulation modes—**balancing and stimulating**), all actions, which the subject of manipulation will make under the influence of transmissions of his **stimulating mode**, will be perceived by him as his own will, his own decisions. Therefore, the subject of manipulation will have to take responsibility for all of his actions. Also, transmissions of **any** of the manipulation modes towards a person completely deprive him of the possibility to soberly evaluate the situation and the manipulator.

In conclusion, it can be added that the effect of even one of the three manipulation modes has a colossal effect on the entire psychophysiology (as "the sum of body and soul") of any person, and application of all modes in manipulation makes this effect many times greater. Any person is absolutely open to this kind of manipulative influence and is defenseless before it.

*****

It goes without saying that this is general introductory information to the topic of influence of natural manipulation modes of *Homo sapiens*. More details about manipulation modes, as well as about what the subject of manipulation feels when his/her **suppression mode** is applied to him/her (in essence, about what sensations force him/her to submit to a manipulator) will be discussed in the second part of this book.

We will only add that a *Homo sapiens* is unable to guess, find out "intuitively" or "feel out" natural manipulation modes; even his own. This means that he cannot control (no matter whom—himself or another person) with a predictable, stable and guaranteed result. In order for this to happen, one should not guess, but instead have information about natural manipulation modes of a person.

This information can be obtained only from the ancient source of knowledge about nature and structure of human psyche, which was named the Catalog of Human Population. And, this is not someone's whim. It is objective reality. If this would not be the case and representatives of the biological type *Homo sapiens* would be able to know themselves and others without any external source, then people in this civilization would not have those problems (for example, with self-knowledge and influencing other people), which they have today. And then, very likely there would be a catalog of human population. However, until recently there were catalogs of anything, but not a catalog of *Homo sapiens*. And, this is a fact.

---

[1] In this case, words "transmit"/"transmissions"/"transmittance" are not used in their regular sense. The term "transmissions of manipulation modes (from the outside)" means a process, in which one person (a manipulator)

influences another person (a subject of manipulation) by using his/her natural individual manipulation modes.

CHAPTER 3

WHAT ARE MANIPULATION SCENARIOS FROM THE CATALOG OF HUMAN POPULATION

In psychology, all existing techniques to manipulate a human essentially are based on "three pillars": collection of information about needs, desires, interests of a subject of manipulation; identification of so-called "targets for influencing" (for example, peculiarities of a person and his needs, satisfaction of which are currently most relevant for him); demonstration of "bait" and encouraging/forcing him to take needed actions. Although this is very primitive, it takes time and considerable efforts, while obtainment of results that a manipulator needs is not one hundred percent guaranteed with this scheme. All this is not required when manipulating a person using his natural manipulation modes from the Catalog of Human Population.

A person, who wants to manipulate someone with a guaranteed result, does not need to collect any information about the subject of manipulation or think about how to influence him/her. There is no need to puzzle over how to behave, look, what to say in order for the subject of manipulation to begin, for example, to feel love all the way up to adoration, deification, worship; or how to make a subject of manipulation your selfless servant, who does not demand anything in return; or how to gain a person's trust, make him think that you are his best friend, even though your attitude toward him and plans for him are very far from friendly; or how to ensure that the subject of manipulation is ready to make any actions, even those, which he would never make voluntarily.

And so on and so forth. The range of what can be done to any person using knowledge of his/her personal natural manipulation modes from the Catalog of Human Population is very, very wide, and all that is necessary is to know the date of birth of the subject of manipulation and to have his/her manipulation scenario (scenarios).

It should be noted right away that by a manipulation scenario we do not mean a literary-dramatic work with a detailed description of actions and lines like for a film production, for example. A scenario of any of manipulation modes of a particular person is detailed information about what kind of person a manipulator must be before the subject of manipulation and how he should act. Or what qualities of personality a manipulator should attribute to the subject of manipulation. A manipulation scenario can be used in different ways depending on a specific objective.

However, first of all, you should know that scenarios of natural manipulation modes of a human are not an invented by someone scheme of actions in relation to a particular person. Any manipulation scenario gets created by developers of the Catalog of Human Population in the same way as they create descriptions of natural programs of a particular subtype of *Homo sapiens* for this Catalog: ancient images from Shan Hai Jing get decrypted for this.

In the third part of this book (chapter titled Suppression Mode Of People Born On October 12th Of Leap Years And October 13th Of Common Years), you can find a specific example of one of the natural manipulation modes of *Homo sapiens*, which was found in the text of the ancient Chinese monument Shan Hai Jing (Catalog of Mountains and Seas) and decrypted.

*****

A scenario of any of human manipulation modes from the Catalog of Human Population (be it suppressing, balancing or stimulating mode) provides details about the subject of manipulation, which can and should be used in manipulation.

Without going into details, a manipulation scenario is essentially a description of a role, which must be acted out by a manipulator in order to get what he needs from another person or a role, which needs to be imposed on the subject of manipulation. A manipulation scenario describes what needs to be done and how to behave in great detail. Typically one manipulation scenario (which is just one out of three human manipulation modes) contains about 20-30 pages of text.

Information in each manipulation scenario is provided on all six factors of human life: intellectual, physical, nutritional, emotional, sexual, and environmental. This range of information about a subject of manipulation allows one to manipulate anyone, at any time. When one has a manipulation scenario of any other person, he can use it in all spheres of human relationships: from every day to foreign policy relations.

For example, the same manipulation scenario can be used by a man to seduce a woman (or another man) or by a subordinate, who decided to get something from his boss; it can be used by a salesman, who wants to sell to something to a customer or by a wife in relation to her husband; it can be applied by parents in relation to their child or by a student in relation to a professor in order to pass a test. And so on.

Now, we will explain what is meant by a manipulation scenario on six factors; we will use application of the suppression mode as an example. A manipulation scenario of the suppression mode provides information on what to talk about, how and what topics to bring up with a subject of manipulation; what values and thoughts to declare, while presenting them as your own; what areas of culture or scientific knowledge to show interest in; etc. That is, it provides information, which can be used to influence the intellect of a subject of manipulation.

Also, a manipulation scenario describes how a manipulator needs to look when meeting with the subject of manipulation: clothing styles and colors, hairstyles, accessories, make-up, perfume, etc. This information is related to the physical factor.

A scenario also describes how to behave if you are planning to have breakfast, lunch or dinner together: what specific dishes and drinks to order for him/her and yourself at a restaurant or cook at home; answers the question of whether or not to cook at home; what the portions should be like; etc. In short, it describes eating habits and algorithms, which must be demonstrated by a manipulator. This information is from the nutritional factor.

Also, any scenario describes emotional reactions, which you need to demonstrate—that is, to act out for a person to whom you are transmitting his/her suppression mode. It also describes the form, in which declared emotions should be expressed. This relates to the emotional factor.

A manipulation scenario also describes how to behave during sexual contact with a subject of manipulation. That is, what types of sex and sexual positions to suggest; what reactions to demonstrate and what sexual preferences to declare, while presenting them as your own. It also describes what specifically to declare in regard to family, children and parents, while presenting these attitudes as your own. This information is from the sexual factor of a subject of manipulation, and it refers to how a woman or a man of his/her dreams (the ideal, which he/she unconsciously seeks) behaves in bed and his or her attitudes towards creation of a family, children, parents.

Also, a manipulation scenario details who to present yourself as to a subject of manipulation in the social aspect (profession, hobby, financial soundness, etc.); how to decorate the interior, if you invited this person somewhere; what kind of gifts to give or offer to give; what preferences to express in terms of the geographical area, climate, housing, interior, vacation, entertainment, etc.; what specific behavioral reactions and algorithms of relationships with others to present as your own. This information is from the environmental factor of a subject of manipulation.

Before the description of all of these six factors, all manipulation scenarios include general information about what kind of individual a subject of manipulation must see in a manipulator in order to begin to obey him and fulfill his demands/requests/wishes. This description helps, as the saying goes, "get into character" in order to play the needed role with maximal effectiveness.

Any person can easily use such a detailed scenario. All that is required is to read the text of a scenario of the suppression mode of a person you want to influence and play the role from this scenario every time you communicate with that person. In case when a manipulator is not able to show some elements from this scenario in reality, be it physical parameters, qualities of personality, skills and knowledge, or material objects—all this can be simply declared using words. That is all. Everything is very simple.

Of course, besides simply playing a role, scenarios of manipulation modes are applied in different ways. However, right now we are not talking about that. What we are talking about is that having complete information about a subject of manipulation (even when you know absolutely nothing about him/her and never met him/her in your life) and having a fully completed plan of what to do, how to behave, how to look, what to say, and so on— from our point of view, is quite convenient. (Not to mention effective.) There is no need to think up anything—simply act and get results.

After all, either way a person, who wants to get something from another person must play some roles for him/her. Is it not easier to know exactly what role to play to whom? Is it not more advantageous to get desired results guaranteed, instead of simply experimenting, spending your time and energy in vain?

In conclusion it can be stated that if a manipulator plays a role according to a scenario, without arrangements, "fantasies" or based on principles like "I want to do it like this", "This is more comfortable for me," etc., then a subject of manipulation will obey him without any resistance; and with all the consequences in the form of material and nonmaterial benefits. However, if someone wants to "remain himself", "self-express" and act as it is convenient for him or as he wants/likes, then it is better for him to forget about achieving any positive results from manipulation; and about influencing others, as well as about the possibility of getting something from them.

Perhaps, some are fine with simply participating in the process and do not need results. However, with the Catalog of Human Population those people, who are not fine with this finally got a chance to stop "pouring" their only life "down the toilet" and can live as they want and get what they need from others.

CHAPTER 4

PARTICULARITIES OF INFLUENCE ON PSYCHE OF *HOMO SAPIENS* USING NATURAL MANIPULATION MODES ADVANTAGEOUS FOR A MANIPULATOR

One of the very advantageous particularities of manipulating a human using knowledge of his individual natural manipulation modes from the Catalog of Human Population is that a manipulator is not just guaranteed to get what he wants from a subject of manipulation, but also he is completely safe from any kind of dissatisfaction, negative reactions, claims from both the subject of manipulation and other people.

The reasons for this are as follows.

The first one is that a manipulator, who uses natural manipulation modes of another person, is always "in the shadows." This occurs because both the subject of manipulation and the surrounding people are incapable of noticing that he is manipulating someone. It is impossible even to suspect that a manipulator is trying to influence someone's psyche, and even more so to accuse him of it.

For example, how is it possible to suspect or accuse someone of manipulation on the grounds that a person ordered a certain dish at a restaurant, wore a particular clothing item or during a conversation said something like "Sometimes I take a shower several times a day and for me any problem with water is an emergency" or "Every morning I go running, but I'm not a sprinter—I am a stayer" or "I very much value that what my parents gave me during my childhood" or "I prefer dishes with plenty of sauce" and so on? This is hard to imagine. And, this means that whatever happens as a result of manipulation of psyche of another person, as the saying goes, "no traces will be left behind." This is very convenient (for a manipulator).

The second reason is that everything that a subject of manipulation was forced to do he explains (to himself and to others) exclusively as his free will, as completely voluntary actions on his part. A subject of manipulation feels a deep inner conviction that he is the only author of those decisions and actions, which in reality he was forced to make. And, there are no suspicions; unlike it often happens with application of traditional methods of manipulation when a subject of manipulation first "swallows the bait" of a manipulator, then realizes this and often not only worries a lot, but also takes revenge on his offender—this is absolutely impossible when using natural manipulation modes.

Thirdly, for the most part, a subject of manipulation fulfills requests/demands of a manipulator with pleasure. The reason for this is that during manipulation the personal suppression mode of a subject of manipulation gets applied, and this mode is a mode of subordination based on the pleasure principle. Against his will a subject of manipulation gets attached to a manipulator, begins to literally love and adore him, and therefore he carries out any action that a manipulator asks him to perform with great enthusiasm. More details about pleasant sensations, which a subject of manipulation experiences during application of his individual manipulation modes can be found in the second part of this book. We hope that this mechanism will become clear to you.

All natural mechanisms mentioned above as an example are very convenient for implementing any kind of manipulation models.

*****

In addition, here is another example of quite a common goal of those, who order from our laboratory information from the Catalog of Human Population about someone's manipulation modes. This example is likely to be of a particular interest to men. Having information about natural manipulation modes, it is possible not only to incline any woman (or man, depending on the sexual orientation of a manipulator) to sex, but also to make her, figuratively speaking, your sex slave for as long as necessary.

In order to get sex men no longer need to spend money on prostitutes or on inclining to sex a person of any gender, age, social stratum. A man does not need to spend money on restaurant outings, gifts, etc.; in short, he does not need to, so to speak, "feed, provide drinks and clothes" if he has information about natural manipulation modes of a person he is interested in. On the contrary, with skillful manipulation of his sex partner (regardless of gender) and having sufficient amount of information about her/him[1], it is possible to motivate a person to share finances with you.

In addition, persuading a sex partner to have any kind of sex that a manipulator likes is also not a problem when you know his/her natural manipulation modes and use them.

What is also important is that if a manipulator uses natural manipulation modes of his partner, then in any sexual contact his physical parameters will not play any role. A manipulator might be not so young, not very healthy, not at all handsome, not have much sexual potency, not have a high social status—his sex partner will still be crazy about him (in the literal sense of the word). And, this charm of a manipulator can last as long as desired—until he himself decides to cut the connection with a subject of manipulation.

If we put aside the possibility of using various witchcraft, magical techniques (known under the words "love spell", "bewitch"[2]) as precedents that do not relate to science, then similar is possible only by transmitting natural manipulation modes of *Homo sapiens* from the Catalog of Human Population. Here, we are talking about purely natural mechanisms, about structure of human psyche; therefore, turning to witches and evil forces is not needed and, very likely, this is important to religious people.

With regard to interests of women, when fully applying manipulation modes to a man, a woman becomes genuinely, passionately loved and cherished for any period of time that she wants. And, she gets from her sex partner (or partners, as any woman, as far as we know, always prefers to have a few of what is called "alternate airfields") absolutely everything she wants. More important is that (just as in the case of men) now in order for a woman to become a real queen, a goddess for someone she also does not need beauty, youth, much of an intellect or possession of large financial means.

Simple arithmetic calculations show that it is much cheaper to purchase information about natural manipulation modes of a man, than to get, for example, plastic surgeries due to the desire to appear younger and more beautiful. After all, an average price of plastic surgeries[3] is between three and four thousand dollars for one fragment of human body, for example, thighs, breasts, tummy, arms, eyelids, lips, etc. In addition to that such surgeries are quite traumatic for a woman's body and can lead to pain and other unpleasant consequences—given a choice, men for whom all this gets done anyway will always prefer young woman; this means that a victim is not solving the problem. A woman who uses a man's individual manipulation modes from the Catalog of Human Population will be loved (and, loved passionately) no matter what shape she is in.

What is also important is that she will be loved for whatever time period she determines herself. In this case, a woman can attach a man to herself forever or for some limited period of time, after which, if she no longer needs this man, she can easily terminate her relationship with him. In order to do this, there is the stimulating manipulation mode. Therefore, it is possible to stop any relationship without damaging yourself and your wallet.

Another benefit for women is that by knowing and applying natural manipulation modes of any man a woman can make him only her own. What is meant here is that a man, who by nature is inclined to polygamy, a woman can very easily turn into an absolutely monogamous partner, who will no longer even think about cheating on her with other women.

We described very briefly some of the benefits that a manipulator gets when he/she applies natural manipulation modes of *Homo sapiens*. The format of this book does not allow to discuss this in more detail. Moreover, it is meaningless to tell about application of natural manipulation modes of a human to people, who never in their lives used this tool on practice. To them everything being told sounds like fiction because they have no personal experience, and therefore do not have an understanding of how this works. We are giving our readers a chance to try this tool for free by providing a scenario of the suppressing manipulation mode of people, who were born on October 12th of leap years or October 13th of common years. Try it and you will see the rest of the benefits for yourself.

*****

In conclusion, we would like to draw the attention of our readers to the fact that by getting only one manipulation scenario of any of the natural manipulation modes from the Catalog of Human Population in order to control someone, a manipulator can apply this scenario to any person, whose date of birth coincides with the date of birth of a subject of manipulation. Meaning that by getting a manipulation scenario of the suppressing mode in order to seduce a specific woman, a man gets a scenario for seducing all women who were born on this date (or dates).

By the way, this is one of the reasons why information about natural manipulation modes of people from the Catalog of Human Population costs as much as it does. By purchasing one manipulation scenario, at once a manipulator receives keys to controlling all representatives of this subtype, and currently on planet Earth there are over twenty million of them (of both genders). This also applies to acquisition of information about an individual program of any person, as it is not someone's personal program, but the program of an entire subtype.

Moreover, if a manipulator has a scenario (or scenarios) of individual manipulation modes of some person from the Catalog of Human Population, then it does not matter to representatives of which race, nationality, gender, social status, and so on to apply this scenario.

Racial, cultural and social differences are secondary; from a purely psychophysiological perspective, the structure of psyche of representatives of the entire human population is principally the same: each person has "software": a natural program and manipulation modes.

[1] "Sufficient amount of information about a person", "having complete information about a person," etc. mean that a manipulator has at least four materials from the Catalog of Human Population about some person; specifically: a complete description of his/her individual (subtype) program, manipulation scenario of the suppressing mode, manipulation scenario of the balancing mode and manipulation scenario of the stimulating mode. Of course, ideally it is desirable to know by which images from Shan Hai Jing all this "software" of a subject of manipulation is recorded in his/her psyche. Since this information also can and should be used on practice; knowledge about images of natural manipulation modes of a subject of manipulation greatly increases the effectiveness of manipulation. An image is always descriptive; it is easy to act it out. Other reasons why it is preferable to have information about images of, for example, manipulation mode, are explained in the second part of this book titled Why A Person Obeys Or Does Not Obey Another Person.

[2] According to esoteric-occult beliefs of a number of people, "to cast a spell" means a magical effect on a person with the goal of causing him to become emotionally and physically attracted to another person. Bewitching is a type of magic that makes a person love someone.

[3] We are referring to prices in the United States of America (2015).

CHAPTER 5

INSTRUCTIONS FOR EXPLOITATION OF *HOMO SAPIENS*

A tool called "natural manipulation modes of *Homo sapiens*" makes it is possible to do anything with human resource of any size. This tool stands out sharply against all other tools currently used by psychologists, managers, marketers, specialists, ideologists, and so on and so forth because it is nothing other than instructions to a human.

The essence of the method of manipulation using information from the Catalog of Human Population is very simple: in order to control people it is necessary to have instructions to them, similar to instructions for household appliances, for example. People are similar to each other only on the outside, but on the inside (meaning from the standpoint of psychical structure) they are different.

To be more specific, it is necessary to have not simply instructions, but instructions for exploitation (use) of a human. Manipulation scenarios from the Catalog of Human Souls are precisely those instructions. Moreover, they are "instructions from a manufacturer."

We hope that there is no need to explain why instructions are necessary, as any modern person knows well that in order to operate even the simplest modern technology he needs to familiarize himself with instructions and act strictly according to requirements provided there. With regard to technology, it would not occur even to an idiot to try controlling, for example, an aircraft without familiarizing himself with instructions. And, as it has long been known, *Homo sapiens* is more complicated than an airplane.

*****

We suppose that many people know the dangers of not having detailed instructions, including "operating instructions" to *Homo sapiens*. Modern "Mengeles" continue to mangle human bodies in search of desired "management buttons," and marketers continue to obsessively offer one junk product after another. This demonstrates their complete lack of a tool that is capable of having a guaranteed, targeted and predictable effect on a system called "a human." For example, one of the mistakes is that modern "puppet masters" try to influence a human through his physiology or intellect. To put it mildly, this looks very naïve. At least because intellect is not psyche—it is a part of psyche; moreover, it is secondary.

Not only practical psychologists, but also scientists have not been able to uncover the method called "individual natural manipulation modes of a human." If they would have found this method, then today this entire civilization would be arranged quite differently. Wars, acts of terrorism, weapons (including biological), politics, security services, killers, advertisers, motivational psychologist and much more simply would not be needed with this method. However, they exist. Even though any representative of human population (individually or as a group) can be forced to perform any actions or destroyed with a guaranteed result without cheap theatricality and colossal expenses.

After all, manipulation using individual natural manipulation modes of a human (with any result) occurs unnoticeably, it does not cause any counteraction and acts of destruction do not fall under any penal code of any country in the world. And, this method can be applied both to individuals and to entire nations.

Scientists, motivated and funded by "top leaders," have been trying to find exactly such a method for a long time. Before them representatives of, for example, religious confessions have been actively looking for this method. At all times the value of this information was so high that all and any tools were used in attempts to obtain it: genocide, wars, inquisitions, sects, concentration camps with experiments a la Dr. Mengele, and so on.

In order to get hold of such a method, for thousands of years innocent people were ruthlessly "finished off": burned, drowned, cut up alive, dismembered, crucified, frozen, forced to survive in cruelest conditions, and so on. Countless numbers of human lives were laid on the altar, but "Mengeles" did not manage to find a single method that would offer individual models of influence on a living system called "a human" (and with a one hundred percent result). All of their attempts more resembled past attempts to study a living cell, which is not visible without a microscope, but when it was put under a microscope—it simply died[1].

While the secret to getting complete control over *Homo sapiens* is very simple: influence should be directed at psyche as a whole. That is—not just at the intellectual or physical factor, but at all six factors: intellectual, physical, nutritional, emotional, sexual, and environmental. And, one should not forget that these six factors, as well as natural manipulation modes are different for each of two hundred and ninety three subtypes of biological type "human."

However, this requires knowledge (down to the details) of what psyche is and what its structure is. And, of course, it is necessary to have knowledge of all two hundred and ninety three individual models of psyche. In other words, the Catalog of Human Population is necessary. However, modern "soul-experts" (psychologists, psychiatrists, anthropologists, sociologists) do not have it.

But all is not so bad. We have the Catalog of Human Population, which is also called the Catalog of Human Souls. As to how we got access to this source of knowledge is a different story. Those who are curious about it can read it in other books in the Catalog of Human Souls series, while this book is devoted to natural manipulation modes.

*****

In the second part of this book, in addition to purely theoretical information that was obtained as a result of research done by the author of discovery of the Catalog of Human Population Andrey Davydov and our colleagues at the laboratory, you will find detailed examples of how natural manipulation modes influence any person. And, it does not matter whether he is an academician of all academies or a super-rich person (whose capital is so great that it would be simply indecent to compare it to capitals of "richest people," for example, from the American magazine Forbes) or one of those "puppet masters," for whom presidents and first faces of countries of the world are just marionettes. Since from a purely natural point of view they are arranged just like all other people.

We think that after reading the next chapters of this book any more or less sane and sensible person will understand why and what for the following inscription appeared in the Temple of the god Apollo at Delphi: "Nosce te ipsum" ("Know thyself"). After all, it only seems to people that they already know themselves. In reality they are just a "poorly cooked" product as the sum of upbringing by their parents, education, cultural and ideological influences, and their own fantasies. They do not exist as individuals; and, not only due to that they do not know their true nature and that they do not know themselves.

However, now this is only half the trouble. If you do not want to know yourself—carry on. No problem, continue living like a zombie and in fantasies about who you are and what you are. The problem is that now you will no longer be able to live quietly, peacefully, calmly and safely in your fantasies because with the discovery of the Catalog of Human Population—human soul (psyche) became, so to speak, public domain, a public place. And, if a person refuses to know how he is arranged by nature, then anyone can freely enter his soul like any public place and do whatever he wants there.

If you still have not understood—natural manipulation modes of *Homo sapiens* are part of the structure of human psyche (soul). Knowing his individual manipulation modes from the Catalog of Human Population (meaning, his personal "instructions for exploitation"), a person eventually becomes capable of noticing any attempts to manipulate him (by any methods, including traditional). Yes, even if a *Homo sapiens* knows his manipulation modes he will still react to them. This is how nature arranged it. However, a person at least gets the opportunity to stop being a marionette in the hands of others.

This is one more benefit of having "instructions to a human." And, we think it is the most important benefit. After all, what is the point of manipulating someone if a manipulator is not even able to control himself and is subject to manipulative influences from the outside just like those whom he manipulates? We do not discuss this in detail in this book, but we hope that any more or less sober-headed reader is able to guess that just as easily and effectively as he/she can potentially use natural manipulation modes of *Homo sapiens* to make others submit to him/her, in the same way he/she also can become one hundred percent controllable using the same tool.

By the way, over twenty years of experience working with users of the Catalog of Human Population, who applied and apply natural manipulation tool for managing, clearly showed that a person not familiar with his own "software," part of which are his/her personal manipulation modes, will never become a truly effective manipulator. Perhaps we will tell about why this is so some other time.

---

[1] Despite its unique characteristics all electronic microscopes had one significant drawback—when living cells and tissues were put under such microscope they immediately died.

CHAPTER 6

WHY A HUMAN SUBMITS TO TRANSMISSIONS OF HIS MANIPULATION MODES

As already mentioned, regardless of gender, race, nationality, etc., from birth any representative of the biological type *Homo sapiens* has manipulation modes, which are required for a variety of psychophysiological processes in an organism. The principle of manipulation of *Homo sapiens* using individual manipulation modes is based on this natural mechanism: "Give a person what he needs, and he will give you what you need."

Due to scientific discovery made by Russian researcher-sinologist Andrey Davydov that *Homo sapiens* is bio-robot and that the Catalog of Human Population exists, it became possible to find out what natural needs are implanted by nature in the unconscious of a particular person and to use this in manipulation of this person; to be able to, as the saying goes, "make offers that cannot be refused," that is—to offer a person that what is vitally important for him. This manipulative technique worked at all times and on absolutely any individual—that is just how a human is arranged.

Natural manipulation modes are natural needs of any human organism, and hence the reactions to their transmissions, which arise at the level of unconscious instinctive reactions that turn a person into an obedient machine for execution of another person's will.

*****

Obtainment of a one hundred percent successful result when using natural manipulation modes of *Homo sapiens* is caused by that these modes are food, a necessary element for normal functioning of any person's organism. Qualities, properties, algorithms implanted in images of natural manipulation modes feed the entire human psychophysiology. Without this "food" human organism is simply not able to function normally.

This food is peculiar, but it is so important for human life that even if a *Homo sapiens* does not know that he has manipulation modes—he instinctively, unconsciously searches for elements of his manipulation modes in the environment throughout the day. In order to obtain qualities and characteristics of his natural manipulation modes, *Homo sapiens* use every sphere of human activity: daily life, work, interaction with other people, culture, various life situations, and so on.

One can fantasize on this topic as much as he wants, but any person does not just do something for no reason, does not just seek something for no reason, does not just love (hate) someone for no reason, do not just eat something for no reason, does not just say something for no reason, and even does not just look at something for no reason. Everything that in one way or another attracts a person's attention necessarily contains elements of his individual program or his personal (subtype)[1] natural manipulation modes—a human is a bio-robot.

Everything else that is not related to his natural "software"—*Homo sapiens* either pays no attention to or pays attention when forced to, but it leaves him untouched, does not cause a deep inner interest and response. And, we think that this phenomenon is easily observable. Every person can test this to make sure. You will see that any person has a clear range of interests on all six factors (intellectual, physical, nutritional, emotional, sexual and environmental) and anything that falls outside this range does not interest a person.

However, the trouble is that due to this natural arrangement, those people, who live without the Catalog of Human Population, and therefore without knowledge of their natural manipulation modes more often than not become easy prey for manipulators. And, not only because they are simply not getting, figuratively speaking, "a multi-dish dinner" systematically in the form of "food" from their manipulation modes on all six factors. People in a civilization without the Catalog of Human Population experience psychological hunger because they are not getting elements of their natural manipulation modes from the environment, and as a result it is possible to say that they get dystrophy; in this sense like dystrophy observed in prisoners of Nazi concentration camps, who did not have enough food.

In this sense, it is possible to feel only pity for *Homo sapiens*, as without enough food called "natural manipulation modes" all of them without exception are not only unhappy[2], but they are also completely dependent on other people, they are not free. Hence, ridiculous statements like: "It is impossible to live in society and to be free from society"[3].

Without having access to the Catalog of Human Population in order to find out their natural manipulation modes[4], people of this civilization are forced, conditionally speaking, to gather them bit by bit—a little bit here, a little bit there; hence, such a powerful effect from transmissions of natural manipulation modes by a manipulator. Sensations and reactions of a person meeting a manipulator, who knows all three of his natural manipulation modes (suppressing, balancing and stimulating) are equivalent to states and reactions of a person dying of starvation getting fed in a posh restaurant or, to be more precise, being invited to dine with a Chinese emperor, on whose table, as it is known, one hundred and eight different dishes get served. Any hungry person simply has no chance to refuse such an offer.

This answers the question why a *Homo sapiens* submits to a manipulator, who transmits his individual natural manipulation modes.

*****

In conclusion we can say that if an individual knows his natural program and his natural manipulation modes from the Catalog of Human Population, it is very, very difficult to make him a subject of manipulation. And, at some point, it is impossible at all. This happens because a person, who knows his natural manipulation modes, is able to provide this "food" for himself and to do it consciously, have control of this process and get that what his psychophysiology needs without pathological dependence on anyone.

However, if a person does not have this information about himself, then at a purely unconscious level, he begins to look for carriers of psychological properties of his individual manipulation modes in the social environment, among family, friends, acquaintances, at work and so on, but he finds ... a manipulator, who is familiar with the Catalog of Human Population and with his/her personal manipulation modes from this Catalog.

*****

In the second part of this book you will learn about another main reason why natural manipulation modes have such a powerful effect on human psychophysiology and make an individual obey a manipulator. Very briefly we will tell about the influence of images through sensations, as well as about what a natural image is and how it differs from an artificial image (including the difference in degree of influence on *Homo sapiens*). And, finally, we will provide two examples from our scientific research base. The first example will demonstrate in detail what a subject of manipulation experiences when a manipulator transmits his/her individual (subtype) manipulation modes toward him/her and on what basis he/she submits to a manipulator. The second example is a description of the process and the results of attempts to influence a person using artificial images.

[1] We would like to draw attention of those readers, who have not yet understood that any element of natural "software" of a human, which we are telling about, essentially is not "personal", "individual" even when called by these words, as both natural program and natural manipulation modes are always not personal, but of an entire subtype. After all, each person is a representative of one of two hundred and ninety three subtypes. We use the word "individual" ("personal") in relation to manipulation modes only to emphasize that there are no common (universal) manipulation modes, as each person has his/her own, personal modes, by the use of which he/she becomes completely controllable.

[2] As it turned out in the course of many years of research of psychical structure of *Homo sapiens*, the state (feeling) called "happiness" directly depends only on one thing—satisfaction of natural needs of a human. And, from birth all needs of *Homo sapiens* are determined by his/her individual natural program and personal manipulation modes. For this reason, no matter how many artificial needs marketers and their ilk think up for a human— satisfaction of these needs does not bring (and, in principle, cannot bring) real satisfaction or a real feeling of happiness.

[3] A well-known saying "It is impossible to live in society and to be free from society" belongs to a famous Russian politician Vladimir I. Lenin (article Party Organization and Party Literature, 1870-1924).

[4] As already mentioned, it is impossible for *Homo sapiens* to "intuitively know," to guess his natural manipulation modes. The only way to get this information is to look in a collection of descriptions of natural "software" of human population—the ancient Chinese text Shan Hai Jing (Catalog of Mountains and Seas), which turned out to be the Catalog of Human Population.

PART 2

WHY A PERSON OBEYS OR DOES NOT OBEY ANOTHER PERSON

Sketch © 2000 Andrey Davydov

CHAPTER 1

SENSATIONS ARE THE BASIS FOR CONTROLLING. IMAGES ARE THE BASIS OF SENSATIONS.

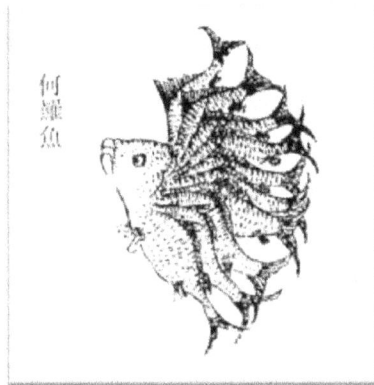

In order to control *Homo sapiens* with a one hundred percent result, the influence should be made not on consciousness, not on intellect, but on the instinctive sphere, on the unconscious. And, it seems that this is not a secret for anyone. However, in this civilization there are big problems with practical application of this knowledge. Since without knowledge of images of natural "software" ("soul") of a person it is practically impossible to realize this on practice.

No matter if someone wants this or not, the unconscious of a person is not controlled by artificial schemes. The language of the unconscious is images and sensations.

Control of human sensations is the basis of power. Here is a primitive example: give a person exactly the same sensations as he was given as a child by mother and father, do it once, twice, ten times and he is yours.[1] Put any command under sensations and a person will perform. And, he will do it at the level of a reflex, without thinking, just like Pavlov's dog[2].

However, it turned out that things are not so simple when it comes to sensations. Each person needs special kind of sensations, individual. A common method of "trial and error" does not work in this case. The method "let's think up an image, one for all" does not work either. If you do not know this, then attempts to control *Homo sapiens* will never have a one hundred percent guaranteed result.

Images, which wild imagination of a manipulator provides are not suitable for management at this level. This civilization already made certain of this and for this reason it required "Mengeles"[3], who rudely break into physiology and psyche of a human using rough, violent, Neanderthal methods. Only a Neanderthal, who does not know how to turn on a computer, can think of beating on it with a hammer. Many "researchers" like Dr. Mengele tried to do the same thing, did they not?

As for images that cause sensations (including sensations that force one person to unquestioningly obey another person), we are not referring to images that are artificial, thought up, modeled, which people of this civilization are used to dealing with. In order to gain total power over any person it is necessary to have information about natural images, by which human "software" is recorded. However, it is not enough to simply open the Shan Hai Jing, as the source that contains all this information about any person—it is also necessary to know which images from this book relate to which particular person.

Using artificial images it is possible to cause, so to speak, "sensations from the head"[4], that is—from intellect, but, strictly speaking, they cannot be called sensations. Natural sensations, emotions, states that arise not from intellect, but from body can be caused only by natural images.

Since modern *Homo sapiens* do not know what to do with themselves, and therefore are obsessed with gaining power through influencing other people (although true power has nothing to do with this), but at the same time it is impossible for the general public to find any information about what "an artificial image" and "a natural image" are, we have to say a few words about this. After all, in essence, an image is the main subject of our scientific research related to the study of the ancient Chinese monument Shan Hai Jing (which turned out to be the Catalog of Human Population) and natural "software" of *Homo sapiens*.

---

[1] You can read about why this is so and what this can lead to in the thirst part of the first book in the Catalog of Human Souls series (the chapter is titled Ahnenerbe: Your Killer Is Under Your Skin (by A. Davydov, O. Skorbatyuk). It tells about how in the absence of a source for obtaining knowledge about natural "software" of *Homo sapiens* mothers and fathers in this civilization (as well as people who act in their place) are forced to, using the computer terms, "install" artificial "software" in their children, which has an incredibly damaging effect on human psychophysiology. In

the context of the book about management, we can add that at the basis of zombiing-pleasant sensations "from childhood" is a simple program: if you do not do like your mother and father taught you—you will die. Intoxicated with the charm of pleasant sensations from childhood, people do not notice how the way of life imposed on them by their parents is killing them. And, it is killing them in reality, not in their imagination, where a recording "if you disobey your mother you will die" is preserved.

[2] Ivan P. Pavlov is a Russian scientist, the first Russian Nobel laureate, a physiologist, the founder of science about higher nervous activity. At the beginning of the XX century, he experimented on dogs. In the Russian language, the phrase "Pavlov's dog" became widely used and it means a person, who acts according to a reflex, without using his intellect.

[3] Josef Mengele is a German physician, who conducted medical experiments on prisoners of the Auschwitz concentration camp during World War II. He conducted criminal experiments on prisoners; for example: anatomization of living infants, castration of boys and men without use of anesthetics, experiments on women, who were exposed to high voltage shocks to test their endurance, and so on and so forth. People who survived after these experiments were put to death. Tens of thousands of people became Mengele's victims.

[4] Sensations are a psychophysical process, which is the psychical reflection of separate properties and conditions of the environment that occur with a direct influence on senses, differentiated perception of internal and external stimuli and irritants by a subject with participation of the nervous system. Psychology separates sensations, emotions and feelings. However, from our point of view, there are no simple states like sensations or complex states like feelings. Contrary to distinction between concepts "sensations", "emotions", "feelings" accepted in psychology, we do not separate them and call them using a single word— "sensations." And, we clearly draw a line between emotions and intellect; hence we make a distinction between "sensations (emotions) from the body" and "sensations (emotions) from the head (intellect)." Distinction between natural emotions (sensations), as signals that come from the body in response to a particular internal and external irritant, and "emotions from the head" we consider fundamental.

CHAPTER 2

IN THE BEGINNING THERE WAS AN IMAGE

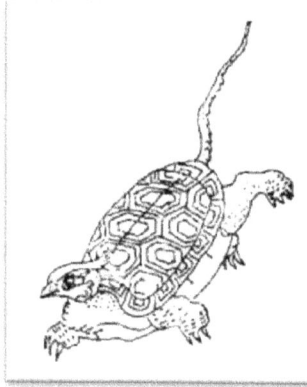

According to historical data, ancient priests knew and actively used an extremely effective tool to influence the masses. The name of this tool is an image.

And, as it is known, priests were the most influential caste in any society. Monarchs, leaders, princes, not to mention simple people obeyed them. With this tool, priests had unconditional, undivided and unlimited power over separate individuals, as well as over entire nations. By the way, according to some of the data, using the tool called "an image" they had the ability to influence even Mother Nature itself.

Ancient priests had such unsurpassed might and such an incredible influence on absolutely any material objects, including humans, only because this influence was based on the natural strength—an Image, which is the cornerstone, the foundation of all things.

To paraphrase the Bible, in the beginning was not a Word, in the beginning was an Image. And, our scientific research confirms this. A human does not think in words, he thinks in images. Words are simply a tool to describe and transmit images that appear in the human brain and nothing more than that. Behind each word spoken by a person (including within himself) is an image. As it is known, *Homo sapiens* are not born with knowledge of some language, they learn languages; not being able to hear human speech (as it is the case with people, who are deaf or deaf-mute from birth) does not prevent from thinking.

*****

Ancient sources also confirm that in the beginning there was an image. We will provide an example of one of these sources. It is available to anyone and many are already familiar with it. It is the well-known ancient Chinese treatise 道德經 Tao Te Ching[1]. It belongs to the category of written sources, which appeared long before the Bible and dates back to VI-V centuries BC. The authorship is attributed to the ancient Chinese philosopher Lao Tzu (老子 "old infant").

According to this source, an image is the basis of all things. However, this is not too obvious because even though no one hid or destroyed Tao Te Ching (as it happened with other ancient books, such as the lost Book/Canon of Music)—there were created so many unintelligible interpretations and commentaries[2] to it (which are far from its true content) that the meaning and the purpose of this book at some point became inaccessible even for the Chinese themselves.

Tao Te Ching is so popular that sometimes it is impossible to distinguish between thoughts of the author of this treatise from interpretations made by its readers, who got inspired by this text. However, due to all this and, from our point of view, due to incorrect translations of this book from Chinese, Tao Te Ching ended up in the category of plainly useless books. Just like everything that brings to an impasse and is unclear, Lao Tzu's treatise began to cause irritation even in professional sinologists. As for non-specialists, simple people—when they read existing translations of Tao Te Ching, commentaries and interpretations it does not even occur to anyone to consider this text as a recipe that can and should be used in daily life. Moreover, it should be used by anyone who wants, not just by those, who are called "the initiated."

Debates about the content of this ancient treatise and its author still continue. However, long-term research done by researcher-sinologist Andrey Davydov, our laboratory's supervisor and the author of the scientific discovery of the Catalog of Human Population, showed that Tao Te Ching along with some of the other ancient books (for example, 易經 I Ching, better known as the Book of Changes[3]), is nothing other than an annotation, meaning a brief description of content and purpose of the ancient source Shan Hai Jing (Book/Catalog/Canon of Mountains and Seas) as the Catalog of Human Population.

Back in the late XX century, Andrey Davydov wrote about this discovery that he made and presented it at scientific conferences, etc. As a sinologist, who understands the mentality of the Chinese and knows that representatives of this nationality especially stand out by that they are very specific and pragmatic, it was difficult for him to come to terms with that sayings of Lao Tzu are amorphous. Hence, an idea was born not to consider this work separately from other ancient books and first of all from Shan Hai Jing, which, as Andrey Davydov already discovered by that time, is nothing other than the source of knowledge about a human and the structure of his psyche. And, this approach led to success.

Andrey Davydov worked with the text of Tao Te Ching in the language of the original using the technology that he created for decryption of Shan Hai Jing as the Catalog of Human Population, while studying translations of this treatise made by other researchers[4]. The result was that none of the existing translations of Tao Te Ching (including those, which were made by very well-known and respected translators among sinologists) reflected the true essence of what is stated in this treatise. However, that is a different topic. What we are talking about right now is that as a result of analysis of hieroglyphics from Tao Te Ching, researcher Andrey Davydov found out that the author of this treatise, whoever he was, in this book actually tells what "an image" is, as the basis of everything that exists in the world we live in, and how this knowledge can be used on practice to transform inner qualities of psychophysiology.

According to conclusions made by Andrey Davydov and recorded in some of his scientific works[5], in Tao Te Ching an Image is regarded as the cornerstone—Tao (Dao) births an image, which precedes the Primogenitor, and so on. This is confirmed by other researchers as well. For example, in translation of Tao Te Ching[6] made by one of the respected Russian sinologists Anatoly E. Lukyanov, the following is stated in zhang (chapter) 21:

> "*Dao is something vague, indistinguishable!*
> *Oh, indistinguishable! Oh, foggy!*
> *On the inside It contains images.*"

An image as a hologram carries information compendiously, multidimensionally through space and beyond time.

Andrey Davydov's understanding of what "an image" is coincides with the opinion of other researchers of Tao Te Ching, who state that Tao is something invisible, but permeating all things, like, for example, magnetic fields or gravitational waves, but even more fundamental; that it is a kind of abyss of singularities that makes up the creative force of existence in our Universe; that it is the source of all forms, the energy that forms the entire process of creation and a creation itself, the creative spirit, which creates and destroys; that the action of Tao is unnoticed and omnipresent and that Tao is everywhere and in everything; that each thing and being, including a human, has its own Tao and own way. And so on and so forth.

However, except Andrey Davydov none of the researchers of this treatise ever stated that Tao Te Ching is the annotation to Shan Hai Jing as the Catalog of Human Population. And, without this knowledge, as it turns out, it is impossible to not only use the text of Lao Tzu's treatise on practice, but even simply to understand the contents of this book.

Sages of the ancient times, who knew how to influence, manipulate people, always faced a dilemma: should those, who will follow them and decide to use the possibilities of Shan Hai Jing as the Catalog of Human Population be warned? From Andrey Davydov's point of view, Lao Tzu tried to leave a description of what awaits a person, who will use this Catalog and what awaits a person, who those will not use it.

Whether the ancient philosopher was forced to write this work or not is not so important, what is important is that he did it. He wrote it for those, who know what it is all about. For those, who do not know anything about Shan Hai Jing as the Catalog of Human Population, to this day Tao Te Ching remains something incomprehensible, impractical, too mysterious and too unclear.

In conclusion of the discussion about Tao Te Ching, according to this source, the natural process of reproduction of images is a perpetual motion. It is impossible to stop it and it is not worth it to even try since it is perpetual. Another thing is that this process births an Image (images), embodying them in us and in other bio-forms living on Earth in its own image and likeness.

*****

However, what does it mean "in image and likeness?" Research done by the author of the discovery of the Catalog of Human Population Andrey Davydov and our colleagues at the laboratory answered this question. An image is a picture, but it is not a simple picture. The essence of the phenomenon called "an image" is in that it is enough to draw some picture (no matter by what means: using paint, a pencil, computer graphics, a photo camera, cinematography or words of fiction, poetry, songs) for a person and this image will begin to influence him in one way or another.

And, this influence is imperceptible, as it bypasses consciousness and intellect. However, the most important thing is that it influences at the deepest level—at the level of functioning of human cells!

This influence manifests in that an image begins to transform a person from within, including at the physiological level. Through a picture, an image inputs into a person that functionality, which it carries in itself. Using an analogy with computers once again, an "installation" of a certain add-on application occurs. A person might not be aware of this (and usually he is not), but this program inside him might "start up" at any moment. And then, like a zombie a person automatically begins to act according to functionality embedded in the image. As it turned out, this process is behind the mysterious "in image and likeness."

In spite of such a powerful and total influence of an image on *Homo sapiens*, if someone particularly curious decides to find out what it is and what modern research of this topic exists—it is unlikely that he will find reliable and comprehensive information about what "an image" is; at least not in sources for the general public.

However, in the age of the Internet some information manages to leak; for example, about that according to research done by geneticists, the language of cells of the human body is a kind of "video", "videotapes"[7]. And this is nothing other than images. Therefore, an image really does influence a human on a cellular level.

*****

As for results of our scientific research, as already mentioned in the first book of the Catalog of Human Souls series titled *Homo Sapiens* Are Bio-Robots. Human "Software," our laboratory's supervisor Andrey Davydov found out that the natural biological program of *Homo sapiens* (or, using the computer terms, "software", which is usually called by the word "psyche", "soul") is recorded by images.

Among other things, an image is the language of human "software." In turn, this "software" is the basis of life and functioning of any person.

As it turned out, a human and a computer have a similarity—both do not work without "software." A computer without software is a useless pile of metal, and *Homo sapiens*—a body that is not able to function as a human. Human body like computer hardware functions only because "software," meaning psyche, works on the inside. Psyche is primary, physiology is secondary.

Today almost everyone is familiar with computer software, but few are familiar with human "software." However, knowledge of humanity in these matters does not influence the existence and functioning of this natural mechanism in any way. Natural "software" works in each representative of the biological type *Homo sapiens* from birth, regardless of whether he is aware of it or not.

Images, as the language of human "software," set the program of functioning of the entire life of a person; in the smallest details, down to what cufflinks for a shirt or lipstick of what color he or she will buy, what he/she will eat for lunch, how he/she will sit, what he/she will wear, what he/she will think, sensate, say in what situations, and so on.

In nature there is a huge number of images as "applications" for a computer called "a human." If you open Shan Hai Jing, at the end of one of its sections (Catalog of the Mountains) that describes natural "software" of *Homo sapiens* at the first level (with which he is born) you can see the number 15,503. This is the number of images (total), by which programs of two hundred and ninety three subtypes of human population are recorded.

However, images can be different. Shan Hai Jing lists natural images, and programs in the human unconscious also are recorded exclusively by natural images; but, artificially created images exist as well. Any artificially created images are fatally harmful for a living system called "a human" and it is possible to find out why this is so from the third part of the first book this series (the chapter is titled Ahnenerbe: Your Killer Is Under Your Skin). After all, as mentioned above, any image (natural or artificial) influences a person at the cellular level. Since, figuratively speaking, a human cell is a soldier and unquestioningly obeys orders of the Image-general; deciding, which image is harmful or useful for a human is not part of its natural functions. A cell is simply a performer.

The evidence of that a *Homo sapiens* really is a bio-robot, whose "software" is recorded by images and that an image is the basis of human existence, life and functioning of any kind are quite detailed descriptions of people, who researchers have never met and do not even know about their existence. These descriptions are not "classified material"—in 2013 they were put on public display at Smashwords.com in a series of two hundred and eighteen books in Russian under the title *Katalog Chelovecheskikh Dush: Programmnoye Obespecheniye Dushi Muzhchin/Zhenshchin, Rodivshikhsya <Data>* [Catalog of Human Souls: Software of Soul of Men/Women Born On <Date>] (by A. Davydov and O. Skorbatyuk)[8]. Essentially, all that was done by developers of the Catalog of Human Population Andrey Davydov and Olga Skorbatyuk in order to get these descriptions was the following: they simply opened Shan Hai Jing and decrypted those archaic images, which this source contains.

Veracity of descriptions mentioned above was verified as a result of experiments in Russian scientific institutions back in the 90s of the XX century and, most importantly, confirmed by over twenty years of practical use of the Catalog of Human Souls (a popular name of the Catalog of Human Population). This means that an image is really the basis of existence of each one of us, *Homo sapiens*.

*****

The point of view that we stated in regard to what "an image" is and how it influences the entire human psychophysiology is confirmed not only by ancient sources, but by modern scientific research as well.

For example, in one of his speeches Harun Yahya, the president of the Science Research Foundation in Istanbul, said that everything we see, feel, hear, and call matter or the Universe, in essence, are only electrical signals reflected from some external objects or sources of energy, which get transmitted to the human brain and form visual, gustatory, tactile, olfactory or audio information in it. He claims that this has long been proved by scientists.

And, as it is known, the human brain forms images as a tool that helps a person remember and keep in memory everything that he ever saw, heard, smelled, felt. These images get imprinted in the brain in the form of pictures (images) and stored in some, so to speak, archives, "files," and this corresponds to one of the scientific hypotheses that the whole world is a big computer and its creator is a programmer.

This hypothesis was put forward not by us. For example, in one of his interviews Dr. Oktar Babuna, M.D., who specializes in neurosurgery, stated that many facts prove the existence of a force (being), which created everything on our planet, including a human. According to his words, using some complex mathematical calculations he proved that any objects in the Universe interact with each other instantaneously, regardless of the distance between them and, in his view, this means that some force that controls everything exits in the world. He justified his theory and then confirmed it experimentally using formulas. According to him everything is calculated in the world we live in, like in a computer game: from the speed of movement of clouds to fate of each person. And, Oktar Babuna is not the only researcher, who came to similar conclusions.

*****

This is a short answer to the question of what "an image" is according to results of our scientific research. An image, as a fundamental natural phenomenon, must be detailed in a separate book, not in a popular science book, and probably not in a single book. However, since the process and, most importantly, results of control of psyche and physiology of *Homo sapiens* depend specifically on the influence of a natural force called "an image"—we had to tell a little bit about this.

Before we share the results of our experiments and tell in detail about the influence of natural and artificial images on a human in the process of manipulation, it is probably worth it to briefly tell about what natural and artificial images are. Since our readers will not find the answer to this question either; at least not in open, public sources.

[1] Tao Te Ching (traditional Chinese: 道德經; The Book of the Way and Virtue) is a fundamental source of teaching and one of the outstanding monuments of Chinese thought, which made a great influence on the culture of China and the entire world.

[2] Allegedly, the total number of classical commentaries to Tao Te Ching is seven hundred, of which three hundred and fifty are preserved. The number of comments in Japanese is two hundred and fifty.

[3] I Ching (traditional Chinese: 易經; The Book of Changes) is considered to be the earliest of Chinese philosophical texts; traditionally it is dated back to about 700 BC.

[4] Currently, over a dozen of translations of Tao Te Ching are published in Russian alone (by Yan Khin-Shun, E. A. Torchinov, I. S. Lisevich, A. A. Maslov, I. I. Semenenko, G. A. Tkachenko, A. E. Lukyanov, B. B. Vinogrodskiy, A. Kuvshinov, V. T. Sukhorukov, A. P. Savrukhin), including four poetic (K. D. Balmont, V. F. Pereleshin, S. N. Batonov, L. I. Kondrashova). Already for over a century and a half, in Europe, America, Russia this treatise is considered the greatest works of Chinese philosophy and attracts attention of the greatest thinkers and cultural figures (H. D. Thoreau, A. Schweitzer, H. K. Hesse, K. T. Jaspers, V. S. Solovyov, L. N. Tolstoy, and others.)

[5] This scientific article by Andrey Davydov has not been published yet.

[6] Lao Tzu. A. E. Lukyanov & V. P. Abramenko (Trans.) *Kanon Dao i De (Dao de tszin). Prozoritmicheskiy perevod s drevnekitayskogo i issledovaniye A. E. Lukyanova, poeticheskiy perevod V. P. Abramenko* [Canon Tao and Te (Tao Te Ching). Prose-Rhythmical Translation from Ancient Chinese and Research by A. E. Lukyanov, Poetic Translation by V. P. Abramenko]. (2008). Moscow: Stilservis, Institute of the Far East of Russian Academy of Science, research society Tai Chi.

[7] Although some researchers-geneticists (for example, Peter P. Gariaev, the creator of the theory of wave genome) for some reason are persecuted in the scientific community, are included in the lists of representatives of pseudoscience, mad people, and so on.

[8] Those, who does not speak Russian, but want to confirm that descriptions made by developers of the Catalog of Human Population exist or want to get information about any person there are interested in from this Catalog in their native language can visit the official website of the Special Scientific Info-Analytical Laboratory—CHS and the Human Population Academy at http://www.humanpopulationacademy.org and order the materials.

Contact information is available on the website, as well as in the Preface and at the end of this book. Also, anyone can familiarize himself/herself with short excerpts from descriptions of natural programs of *Homo sapiens* in the second book of the Catalog of Human Souls series titled Hack Anyone's Soul. 100 Demos Of Human Programs From The Catalog Of Human Population.

CHAPTER 3

WHAT ARE NATURAL AND ARTIFICIAL IMAGES

As it was already mentioned in the previous chapter, according to results of our scientific research, an image is the language of "software" of *Homo sapiens*. What do we mean by this?

Images (individual archetypes of the unconscious[1]) make up the structure of human psyche; they are segments-"bricks" of individual archetypal pattern[2] or, in simple, non-scientific language—of natural programs and manipulation modes. Images are responsible for personal qualities, functioning and lifestyle of an individual and provide interaction between his psyche and physiology.

It should also be noted that by images, as the language of "software," firstly, we mean individual, not collective archetypes of the unconscious of *Homo sapiens*; secondly—only those specific images that are contained in the text of Shan Hai Jing; and thirdly, only natural images. According to results of our research, all other images are not images of human unconscious, human "software."

Using the language of scientific psychology, images are archetypes of the unconscious of *Homo sapiens*, but in the case of non-traditional psychoanalysis, which bases on information about natural "software" of a human from Shan Hai Jing—these archetypes are not collective, but are individual. According to the Shan Hai Jing, collective archetypes[3] have no relation to natural "software" of a human, as they relate to artificial "software."

Since in this civilization either little is known or little is told about an image as such, we will briefly tell about what natural images and artificial images are.

However, in this chapter we will not go into details of this interesting and important topic for each one of our readers because this matter does not fit the format of the book and because all of the most important things concerning natural and artificial "software" of *Homo sapiens* are already described in our other books[4]. In the format of this book, it is enough to get an idea about the difference between artificial images and natural images because success of a manipulator's actions depends on this.

*****

First of all, a **natural image** is an image that was not created by human imagination.

Natural images are images of any object of animate and inanimate nature (in a chimeric combination as well[5]) that exist in reality, as well as some mythological images—those, which are recorded in Shan Hai Jing. Natural images are the language of "software" of *Homo sapiens* because they have a particular influence on human psychophysiology. Any artificially created image (meaning, an image thought up by a human) does not have such powerful influence as any natural image has.

For those people, who wish to familiarize themselves with natural images we recommend opening the Shan Hai Jing (Catalog of Mountains and Seas) in their native language and see with their own eyes what natural images are.

Do not be disconcerted by that natural images of "software" of *Homo sapiens* in Shan Hai Jing might look somewhat fantastic and that they might differ from objects of animate and inanimate nature, which we see around us. For example, a fox might have not one, but nine tails; instead of one head, a bird might have two or more heads; the body of a bull might be joined with the body of a fish and at the same time might have, for example, the head of a tiger and the tail of a snake.

Despite this, all images from Shan Hai Jing are exclusively natural images. And, these natural images look so strange and unusual because essentially any image of programs and manipulation modes of *Homo sapiens* is a formula; a formula of functionality of a person. For this reason, these images should not be taken literally.

For those people, who want to understand what natural images are in the context of images of human programs are also encouraged to see illustrations to Shan Hai Jing. However, be warned that illustrations that did not come directly from this source might be adaptations of images from

Shan Hai Jing. Such images can be found on the Internet. And, any, even the smallest addition, distortion in a depiction of a natural image automatically turns it into an artificial image. In this sense, the text of this ancient source is a more reliable source of knowledge about what natural images are than someone's drawing.

Artificial images include any image made up by a human, as well as any natural image that he arranged/adapted.

A remarkable and very striking example of arrangement of natural images is any children's toy. For example, a plush toy that has a certain similarity with some real natural object (a bear, a cat, a dog, etc.), but contains too many principal differences from the natural analogue. After all, no real bear looks exactly like a toy teddy bear.

Sometimes when looking at a children's toy, at first glance it is impossible to tell what is in front of you. For example, the upper part of such a "masterpiece" resembles a duck and its feet remind of a toy bear's feet, while in nature no creature has such feet.

Due to such principal differences between a natural analogue in the form of an animal and a children's toy that imitates it—all such toys are harmful to a child's psyche and physiology. Even though manufacturers of these toys, parents, and, especially, children themselves do not know about this. However, this is a different topic.

There are also toys-chimeras; for example, products of the Walrus Toys company called Chimeras Mix 'n' Match Plush—a plush construction set a la Lego. Here, in addition to distortions in terms of form, the manufacturer also introduces distortions into functionality of a particular natural image. For example, a frog is forced to fly by attaching body parts of an owl to it, and so on. Psyche of *Homo sapiens* is chimerical by its structure and perhaps because of this glory of creators of Shan Hai Jing (and not just the book) gives no rest to scientists-geneticists and manufacturers of children's toys. However, such distortion of a natural image has a terrible influence on psyche of children.

All (without exception) artistic images of all (without exception) literary, pictorial art, musical, design and other works created by humans are also examples of artificial images; and, of course, any images from movies, videos, the Internet, except for videos and photographs of natural objects (not arranged by a human). Images created by directors and actors in any film or theatrical production are also examples of images from this category.

In a nutshell, this is what natural and artificial images are. It is very easy to distinguish one from the other—it is enough to simply ask a question: "Was this created by nature or by a human?"

The difference between an artificial and a natural image, figuratively speaking, is the same as the difference between a natural apple and a plastic apple, or between natural leather and leatherette. If a person is forced to eat imitations of food made out of plastic or his body gets fully covered by artificial leather—he will not stay alive for very long. Things are similar with natural and artificial images: any natural image gives life, makes a person healthier, stronger, mightier, and any artificial image weakens psyche and body of a person and slowly kills him.

All artificial images without exception are extremely harmful to human psychophysiology, and for this reason people in this civilization have such a short lifespan. This is the price that a *Homo sapiens* pays for being haunted by the glory of the Creator. On the one hand, desire for creativity is quite natural and explainable since humanity is created "in His image and likeness." However, the fact that is not being taken into account is that humanity still has to grow to the level of the Creator capable of creating natural images.

In the meantime, a human pays with his own health and life for childlike attempts to compete with the Creator. What is the point of such creativity? After all, besides creation of artificial image, a human is able to create masterpieces on the basis of natural images and for this he will not have to die.

*****

Returning to the topic of this book, it is necessary to know that any *Homo sapiens* becomes one hundred percent controllable only if a manipulator uses natural images of a person's manipulation modes for management. Any other images, for example, images of manipulation modes of people that do not relate to the subtype structure of the subject of manipulation or artificial images will never turn a person into an automatic machine, who carries out the will of a manipulator.

If a manipulator wants to control with a one hundred percent guaranteed result, then he must use either scenarios of manipulation modes from the Catalog of Human Population (as images from Shan Hai Jing, which have already been decrypted) or images of manipulation modes. Of course, the latter requires certain knowledge and experience from a beginner and it is more complicated than using manipulation scenarios, but it is also possible. However, simultaneous use of a manipulation scenario and images of the natural manipulation mode of a particular person is most effective when managing/controlling a *Homo sapiens*.

Now, in order to demonstrate how images of a person's natural manipulation modes transmitted by a manipulator influence his psyche, we offer you to familiarize yourself with the description of sensations, which a subject of manipulation experiences during such transmission.

This description is taken from the experimental base related to developments of the Catalog of Human Population, which is already over twenty years old. Based on experiments that were carried out, researchers concluded the following: reactions to transmissions of natural manipulation modes are "like copies," absolutely identical in all subjects regardless of individual's belongingness to a particular subtype.

Materials for this description are provided by our colleagues from the laboratory to be included in the text of this book as examples, so that readers could get at least some understanding of how natural manipulation modes of *Homo sapiens* work. Although in order to fully understand this it is, of course, necessary for each person to have his own personal experience using manipulation modes on practice.

For comparison, Chapter 4 tells what happens to a person towards whom images of his manipulation modes, meaning—natural images, get transmitted by a manipulator and in Chapter 5 we present results of experiments based on application of artificial images in manipulation. This is done so that anyone, who wants to manipulate another's soul could decide whether he/she will continue his/her attempts to control other people using artificial images and get little results, or for the sake of getting real and total power over another person and benefits from manipulation he/she will use the new tool called "natural manipulation modes of *Homo sapiens* from the Catalog of Human Population."

We are simply providing the opportunity to compare results of application of these two methods of human manipulation. And, which one of these methods each of our readers will choose in the end is not our business. Whether our readers will want to use the new tool or not does not concern us. Our position is that in manipulation of people each person has the right to use whatever tool he likes more. Even if the tool that he/she chooses does not work.

---

[1] Images are individual archetypes of human unconscious. However, by "individual archetypes" we mean archetypes of a subtype. On the one hand, "individual archetypes" make up the individuality of a person as a representative of a particular human subtype and distinguish him/her from representatives of all other subtypes of *Homo sapiens*. However, on the other hand, as segments and the language of "software," individual archetypes are the same for all representatives within one of two hundred and ninety three subtypes of the "human" biological type.

[2] In essence, concepts human "software" (which, using scientific terms is the same as "subtype structure" or "individual archetypal pattern"),

"psyche" and "soul" are synonymous. Since we do not want to make texts of our popular science books difficult, instead of the scientific name "individual archetypal pattern" we prefer to use words that are simple and understandable by any reader.

3 In analytical psychology founded by Carl Gustav Jung, an archetype (ancient Greek ἀρχέτυπον – pre-image) means universal innate psychical structures that make up the content of the collective unconscious. According to Jung's perspective, an archetype is a class of psychical contents, events of which do not have their source in a separate individual. Specificity of these contents is in their belongingness to a type that carries properties of the entire humanity as a certain whole. Jung called these types or "archaic remnants"—archetypes.

4 See Part 3 (Ahnenerbe: Your Killer Is Under Your Skin) in the first book of the Catalog of Human Souls series titled *Homo Sapiens* Are Bio-Robots. Human "Software."

5 Chimerism of natural images from Shan Hai Jing is expressed, for example, in conjunction of several animals or a human and an animal, as well as in increase of the number of separate body parts of a particular natural object.

CHAPTER 4

PROCESS AND RESULTS OF CONTROLLING A HUMAN ON THE BASIS OF NATURAL IMAGES OF NATURAL MANIPULATION MODES

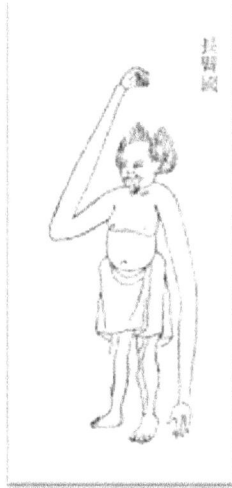

We will try to describe the process, in which one person begins to obey another. The process is described in terms of sensations, which a subject of manipulation experiences when natural images of his/her suppressing mode from Shan Hai Jing get transmitted toward him/her[1].

It is not an easy task to describe what a subject of manipulation experiences during transmissions of his suppression mode. After all, we are telling about this to people, who probably have not yet experienced the influence of suppressing mode on themselves personally, and it is the same as telling about the taste of a dish that a person has never tried. However, we will try.

We think that this description will answer the following question of our readers: why when a manipulator transmits individual natural modes toward a subject of manipulation he obeys him without reservation, without any internal resistance, with pleasure? In parallel, this description will be a good illustration of the statement that we expressed at the beginning of the second part of the book: "Sensations are the basis of power."

Before we proceed with the description, it is necessary to make a note. Despite that during transmissions of the stimulating mode a subject of manipulation experiences the whole spectrum of very bright emotions—the basic emotions in this case are happiness and joy. Hence, pleasure and sexual attraction (excitement) arise. However, do not think that due to this transmission of the suppression mode solves only the problem of finding love or seduction—the appearance of sympathy and strong sexual attraction (usually referred to by the word "love") in a subject of manipulation toward a manipulator is the basis, on which a subject of manipulation submits to him/her and fulfills his/her wishes.

Therefore, suppressing mode should not be regarded only as the mode that causes love and sexual desire. This manipulation mode certainly can be used by a manipulator solely for this purpose. However, arousing "love" and passion is not the only and not the most important property and intended purpose of the suppression mode of *Homo sapiens*.

The main properties and intended purposes of this mode are suppression and subjugation. Pleasure that a subject of manipulation gets from the suppressing mode and his/her "affection" for a manipulator is the basis for suppression and subordination of one person to another. Suppression mode has a very wide spectrum of use. It is applied in absolutely all situations when it is necessary to get on the right side of somebody: from every day or "romantic relationships" to business and international politics.

*****

Now, we will tell about how transmissions of his/her individual suppressing mode influence a *Homo sapiens* of any gender, any race, nationality, age, social status, education level, etc. The text that describes sensations, which a subject of manipulation experiences in this specific case, includes excerpts from reports of subjects, on whom scenarios of suppressing manipulation mode from the Catalog of Human Population were tested and they are presented in the form of quotations.

One of the characteristics of transmissions of the suppression mode toward a person is that regardless of the mood, physical state that he/she was in prior to meeting a manipulator, practically from the very beginning of transmissions he/she begins to experience an increasing sensation of happiness.

"Your suppression mode can cure any psychological wounds regardless of how long you had them and how deep they are. It is as if a wonderful healing, life-giving elixir starts pouring on you at the first "faint notes" of your suppression mode, and with every minute you feel more joyful, happier, your souls becomes more at ease. ..."

"Almost immediately your head if fully freed from painful reflections, memories and any thoughts at all. It is as if the intellect gets turned off, and without any Buddhist meditative attempts to "stop your mind" or stupidifying means like drugs or "psychotropics." ..."

"All heartaches disappear, the soul becomes light as a bird and as if skyrockets, straight to heaven. And, it begins to soar there freely, bathing in gentle gusts of wind and caressing sun rays. The weight of worries, years, and problems disappears as if by a magic wand. ..."

"Your body becomes incredibly relaxed without any muscle relaxants. That in itself is already incredibly pleasant! I noticed that throughout an entire day and sometimes even night modern people are in "a state of a spin," stiffness, twistedness and they experience discomfort and pain because of this. Suppression mode as if untwists this "spin" and you feel at ease and very pleasant. ..."

"It is hardly possible to describe this state with words, but it vaguely reminds of the state of cloudless childhood happiness. Only it is much more powerful and much deeper. I swear, cannot remember being so happy even during childhood, even though it was the happiest time in my life! ..."

"When your suppression mode is transmitted towards you, a wave of happiness almost immediately covers you and completely absorbs you. And, with great pleasure you drown in this incredibly pleasant languor. ..."

The state that a person experiences during transmissions of his/her suppression mode by a manipulator can be compared to the effect of drugs. Although this is not the best comparison, it helps get an approximate idea of described processes, immersion of a person into the deepest sweet happy coma. However, unlike it is with effects from narcotics, a person toward whom his suppressing mode is transmitted can come back to reality at any time[2].

If you observe a subject of manipulation when his/her suppression mode is transmitted toward him/her, and especially when communication with a manipulator is in full swing, you will notice that even though he does not look intoxicated or drunk—his eyes are clouded, his face is lit up with happiness and a blissful smile wanders on it. It is easy to notice that his body is in a very relaxed, comfortable state, and he is, using the language of slang, "catching a buzz."

When communicating with an individual, who is transmitting individual suppression mode of a person, the subject of manipulation immediately falls out of the brutal, traumatizing, unpleasant reality. Time and space as if cease to exist for him/her.

> *"You find yourself in a wonderful fairy-tale dimension that you saw in your dreams many times and where you always felt incredibly well and pleasant. Only in this case you are not sleeping and this fairy-tale world as if suddenly materialized, right here in reality. It became a reality and you can see, hear, touch it, and breathe it in! And, it's not a dream!! ..."*

During transmissions of the suppressing mode toward a person, the surrounding reality recedes into the background for him/her, taking pain, troubles, and problems with it. All worries, sadness, grievances, and fears as if get erased from his memory by a magic eraser. If at this moment you ask a person what torments, annoys, worries him—it is unlikely that he will be able to remember right away.

Unpleasant people, terrible circumstances and situations in the life of a subject of manipulation no longer come up in memory when his/her suppression mode is applied to him/her; it is as if they remain in space from where a person came to this "paradise island" of bliss, peace and joy. By subjective sensations, all of them as if sunk into oblivion, melted like ice cubes in a fireplace.

If at the moment when a person feels happy due to transmissions of suppression mode in his direction you start asking him about difficulties and problems in his life, he will either wave his hand in order to show that there are no concerns or with a blissful smile on his face say: "There are no problems really." And, at that moment this will be the truth. A person does not feel absolutely any discomfort or sufferings, even though most likely things are not so peachy in his/her life.

Being in a wonderful "parallel world" of complete and total happiness, in which a person finds himself when someone transmits his suppression mode is also characterized by that the only person, who the subject of manipulation sees, hears, senses close to him is a manipulator. Even if this takes place in a huge crowd while sandwiched between bodies like in Moscow's metro during rush hour—a person simply does not notice any other people. It is as if they are not there—a person completely stops noticing them.

******

From the state of sweepingly-piercing happiness, gradually and slowly a person sinks into the abyss of pleasure deeper and deeper. In the midst of a joyful, cheerful mood and a blissful state, which already appeared "out of nowhere," desire begins to flare up on the inside.

> *"You start feeling that something pleasantly-viscous fills you up on the inside, and heat begins to flow throughout you whole body. Usually alcohol gives a similar effect, but here it is much stronger. It is as if your whole body begins to glow from this warmth inside of you. And, you begin to feel very joyful because of this caressing "sun" inside you. ..."*

> *"You literally drown in his eyes. You hear only his voice and nothing else. And, this voice has a very powerful effect on you! It pulls you deeper and deeper into a whirlpool of incredibly sweet pleasure. You're happy and you cannot resist giving in to a sudden sweet feeling of attraction to this person. ..."*

> *"You become totally indifferent to the color of this person's skin, his nationality, his age, you do not care whether he is handsome or ugly and how much money he has—you already love him! And, you want him more and more in the sexual sense of the word. ..."*

> *"The feeling of sympathy and sexual arousal sometimes burns like a calm flame, and sometime overwhelms you, just like flames take over a sheet of paper. The heart begins to beat so fast that it feels like it is going to jump out of the chest! Blood literally begins to boil in the veins, the mouth dries up and words get stuck in the throat. ..."*

What is remarkable is that from one meeting with a manipulator to the next, the feeling of sexual attraction that arose toward him/her in a subject of manipulation not only does not stop, but also sexual attraction and excitement increase. This is unusual for regular relationships, in which only novelty really excites. Continuing sexual excitement experienced by a person being manipulated toward a manipulator turns into a sweet, joyful mania.

However, what is characteristic is that every person toward whom his/her suppression mode was transmitted was surprised that the formed attachment to a complete stranger did not worry him/her at all.

> *"You feel very well, very comfortable with your attachment to this person. You feel SO well that with your own hands you are ready to tie the knots on ropes attaching you to a manipulator ever tighter. ..."*

When continuing transmissions of the suppression mode, a subject of manipulation fearlessly flies toward light like a moth as soon a manipulator appears on the horizon.

> *"You feel like a fly that cannot resist trying out sweet juice, which attracts it like a magnet; you cannot resist this attraction. And, you do not want to resist it! ..."*

> *"This great attraction to a manipulator doesn't worry you in any way; on the contrary, with great pleasure you're observing shackles on your hands and feet. ..."*

It is not necessary to persuade, beg or demand a subject of manipulation to do something for the subject of his/her burning adoration—a manipulator. A subject of manipulation is in such a deep state of fascination, in love that like a faithful dog he/she is ready to sit by the feet of a subject of his/her unearthly love (whom he/she subjectively perceives as a deity descended from heaven) his/her whole life.

> *"I want only one thing—to be with this man! Always! Everywhere! At any time of day or night! I want to sit and catch his glances, to drown in his eyes over and over again. For the sake of this happiness you're ready to run at full speed in order to fulfill even a hint of a wish of your beloved, adored, desired. ..."*

> *"Not only every time we meet, but even when a thought about the manipulator arises—you get fully absorbed by wild admiration, overwhelming joy that enter the body through all holes and sweetly torment on the inside. You are ready to do anything, to give everything to her just so that this incredible fairy-tale never ends. ..."*

Notably, tender impulses and wild passions in relation to a manipulator, as well as sweet languor and piercing, inexpressible happiness, which people usually have the opportunity to experience only in childhood, do not disappear when parting with a manipulator. A manipulator leaves and, of course, a subject of manipulation becomes a bit sad, but his/her sweet fairy-tale does not end with this.

Indeed, such pleasant "long-lasting states" probably occur most often with the use of drugs. Only in the case of application of the suppressing mode to a person this pleasure does not kill him, but on the contrary—it gives him the strength to live, revitalizes, restores and fills him with incredible energy.

Sudden warm feelings toward a manipulator are always experienced by a subject of manipulation as the greatest love of his/her life, as the most wild, truly all-consuming passion; and, of course, as the most powerful sensations during sex, if sexual relations took place between a manipulator and a subject of manipulation.

> "It's enough to have sex with a person, who transmits your suppressing mode to you only once in your life and it seems to you that you really were in paradise! ..."

> "No other partner (neither before nor after) ever gave me such feelings during sex. Ever. People say that "first love" is something you remember forever, etc. I couldn't care less about my first love or my thirty-first love, or about all of them combined when THIS woman is beside me!"

> "Actually, I never was a saint and, as they say, I "never missed a skirt." Also, I never fully understood the word "fidelity" because there are so many pretty women around! But, after sex with a partner, who used my suppression mode, I completely stopped even looking at other women!!! This is very strange for me; it is as if I'm a new person! ..."

> "I simply don't know why I'd have sex with someone, who doesn't know my suppression mode, and therefore cannot give me such mind-blowing sexual sensations. ..."

The flame of passion grows and intensifies, and a subject of manipulation is so impressed with new sexual sensations, which were unknown to him before that he begins to crave repetition of sexual relations with a manipulator again and again. Moreover, a subject of manipulation will never become bored with a manipulator, if he continues to transmit his suppression mode. Probably that is exactly the reason why while this sexual relationship continues it will not even cross the mind of a subject of manipulation that it is possible to have sex with someone else.

> "How can changing a partner even come to mind when orgasm during sex with this one is powerful like lightning that strikes a tree?!? ..."

> "Oh, that sweet state after sex, which is like a long-lasting lollipop in your mouth—it seems like it will never end. Although I dreamt of

*this my whole lifetime, I never experienced this with anyone before.
..."*

In short, impressions experienced by a subject of manipulation from transmissions of his suppression mode during sexual contact as such powerful orgasmic sensations were never before experienced by him with anyone else.

> *"I never experienced such mind-blowing sexual sensations with anyone of my sexual partners in the past. I cannot even compare THIS with anything. ..."*

However, this is not surprising. Even if a subject of manipulation found some of his/her previous sex partners suitable, there was always something that irritated and often repulsed. This does not and in principle cannot occur with a manipulator because he/she acts out for a subject of manipulation a man or a woman of his/her dreams.

A man (or a women) from the suppressing mode is a very specific image, type. And, when a subject of manipulation encounters this character type—his (her) unconscious instantly recognizes him: "This is him (her)!!!!" Therefore, a subject of manipulation always perceives and evaluates a manipulator, who plays the role from a scenario of the suppressing mode as an ideal partner; and ideal not in some particular segment of a relationship, but ideal in every way.

Something like this rarely happens in people's lives—dreams remain dreams and with all the sympathy for his/her partner a person has to endure his/her numerous flaws throughout life. In essence, these are not flaws at all, but only discrepancies with an image of "a man (a woman) of his/her dreams" that is imprinted in the unconscious from birth.

Sometimes a person searches for Him or Her ("my great love", "my second half") his/her entire life; searches everywhere and always. Sometimes, seeing a few qualities from his/her suppression mode in someone, an individual immediately literally clings to this person, but ... with time he/she concludes that "No, again this is not Him (Her)" and when they part bitterly says to his/her partner: "I was mistaken about you!" As a result, people either remain alone or live "alone together."

Specifically for this reason, meeting a manipulator, who transmits the stimulation mode, for any person always seems like something transcendental that does not exist in reality. After meeting and having a relationship with a manipulator (especially sexual), at first it seems to a subject of manipulation that it was a dream.

"Before you meet a person transmitting your personal suppression mode, you never met an ideal partner, "the man of your dreams." And, suddenly you meet him; exactly him. At first it's a shock! After all, you could see him only in your dreams and fantasies, but not in real life. ..."

"Real people, whom you met in your life, always disappointed you sooner or later. You meet someone, who seems like the man of your dreams at least a little bit, and then this feeling suddenly melts away like ice. And, when you take a closer look there is only a man, who is not like Him at all. ..."

"You got so used to that there is no fairy-tale in reality and cannot be. And, suddenly you find yourself in a fairy-tale!!! And, in your own, personal fairy-tale, which, as you thought, only you and no one else knows about. This amazes greatly when you meet a person, who is transmitting your suppression mode. ..."

"I think that even a non-religious person will believe in the existence of some Higher power after this. You begin thinking that God or Providence led you to come across the person of your dreams. After all, this never happened before to you personally or to your friends (judging by their stories). And, it is impossible not to believe in the existence of Providence because when you look at the manipulator from all sides—you do not find anything that you do not like in this person. It's truly a miracle! ..."

"Suddenly you meet Her! Real, of flesh and blood!! Your fairy-tale as if comes to you in the guise of a woman, who transmits your suppression mode, and reality recedes somewhere to the background. Yes, at first it is a bit unusual, fantastic, but you simply cannot resist and you jump into this ocean of love head first. ..."

A subject of manipulation, who already accepted that his/her fairy-tale will never become a reality, sometimes cannot right away believe that happiness suddenly fell upon him/her. Therefore, ideally it is necessary to act out a scenario of the suppression mode of a person for some time. A subject of manipulation must fully, as the saying goes, "accept his/her happiness."

Usually, a subject of manipulation initially tries hard to soberly look at a manipulator (although he/she always fails in this because this is impossible in principle) and in different ways tries to ensure that a manipulator really is the one from his/her secret dreams. (This is why for serious manipulation it is necessary to have a complete scenario of the suppression mode, not its short version.)

After getting tired of fruitless attempts quickly enough, a subject of manipulation capitulates and surrenders with pleasure.

> "Questions like "How does she know that this is exactly what I love and that this is just what I want" do not torment very long, as very quickly and with pleasure you forget about them and say to yourself: "Who cares? What difference does it make?!" And then, you just enjoy. ..."

> "You do not think about who she is. Does it matter? Such happiness does not fall on your head every day, does it? And, you just know, you just feel that you are really ready to give your life for this woman. ..."

> "You think that even if you are seeing this man in your sleep—only a stupid woman will want to wake up from this wonderful dream. ..."

> "The only thought that might cross your mind several times is "Oh wow, I never thought that I like women who look like this, are in this age category, of this nationality" or something of that sort. ..."

> "I will say this. After getting surprised a couple of times by your own preferences for women, which you were unaware of (it turns out that I also like this kind of women!!!), you happily forget about the past and again jump into the abyss of a joyous, extremely exciting and inspiring state. You do not care about what was and what will be. You are happy right now! ..."

*****

However, it would be wrong to think that incredible, unusual and absorbing sensations, which a subject of manipulation experiences are limited to only unbelievable happiness, extreme joy and burning sexual passion; even though these states certainly prevail among others when a person's suppression mode is transmitted toward him/her.

For a subject of manipulation, relationship with a manipulator is painted with all colors of the rainbow on the basis of five basic human emotions[3]: joy, aggression, fear, anger, and complete "zero," as a happy emotional "calmness." On the basis of his/her return to the state of cloudless happiness from communication with a manipulator, at times he/she is very joyful and at other times very afraid or terribly angry or suffers greatly. Only one thing is not present—boredom.

Sensations that a subject of manipulation experiences are like a big kaleidoscope—its stones fascinate a viewer because each time he sees a completely new image.

For example, when a manipulator is not near him/her, a subject of manipulation is tormented by terrible anguish. He feels desperately sad, lonely, he is tearful. And, by their nature and intensity these experiences are unlikely to resemble those that he felt when he was separated from any of his partners in the past; regardless of how much he loved someone in the past. After all, the scale and significance of a person, who transmits toward a subject of manipulation his/her suppression mode, can be compared to a star called the Sun: when its light is not shining everything on Earth plunges into darkness and coldness, and in its absence—ceases to exist altogether.

> *"Sometimes when she is not with me it is absolutely unbearable. I never thought that a woman can make me worry about parting with her so much. When my sunshine is not beside me, great anguish comes over me... And then, there is a wild impulse to drop everything and rush to her like the wind. ..."*

> *"I'm so sad, so bitter when he's not near me that I'm either in tears from inability to be with him right now or in a wild rage. At these moments I want to pierce the space like the wind, despite any obstacles that stand on my way to him and go to him wherever he is! ..."*

Indeed, as many years of experiments have shown, the desire of a subject of manipulation to be close to a manipulator, who transmits the suppression mode toward him/her is stronger than the strongest wind, storm or tornado. God forbid someone or something gets in the way of the incredibly strong desire of a subject of manipulation to finally be next to the subject of his burning lust.

> *"On the inside I feel energy of such penetrative power that I never felt until now. When I feel most painful due to that she is not next to me, it is as if I become a whirlwind that can demolish any obstacles, any difficulties that stand in the way of my desire to be with her right now! ... "*

Other people should not even try to think about standing in the way of this person- whirlwind. Even at the hint of an obstacle an individual of any gender toward whom someone is transmitting his/her suppression mode becomes incredibly pushy and aggressive. The best thing that others can do is immediately step aside; of course, if they want to stay alive and healthy.

In terms of power, pressure and possible damages this person really does resemble a tornado or a whirlwind. And, it does not matter who he or she was, so to speak, "in the past life," before meeting a person, who transmits the suppression mode toward him/her: aggressive and assertive or shy and timid—now everything is different. A subject of manipulation literally transforms from communication with a manipulator; such energies begin to boil in him/her that if necessary he/she will tear apart anything and anyone.

Also, just in case, it is recommended to hide everything like guns, knives, etc. from a subject of manipulation, who is eager to get to a manipulator. Since this person is experiencing such a strong desire for the subject of his passion that he might do a lot of things, which he/she will regret for a long time. At the slightest obstacle, he/she literally becomes furious and in a stormy impulse, fearlessly and with compelling power goes into an attack.

*****

Also, sometimes a person toward whom someone is transmitting his/her suppression mode is overcome by wild fear when it simply crosses his/her mind that one day a manipulator might disappear from his/her life forever. He/she literally gets paralyzed with chilling fright just imagine this.

> *"Yes, right now I can say that I'm absolutely happy, but my happiness a bit clouded by the question that haunts me, desperately drills my brain: "Will I be able to live without this woman?" But, no matter how hard I think through various options of my life in her absence, I cannot find one that would be at least somewhat satisfactory. This surprises and worries me greatly. ..."*

> *"I think a lot about what would happen if he disappears from my life. To be honest, simply a thought about this drives me crazy. Why? It is actually very simple: because neither in my circles nor anywhere else there is no one for me, who could replace him! I know this for sure and I don't even want to look someone to replace him! Before, a breakup with a partner never stopped me from opening my heart to new love, new relationships. This is a bit scary. ..."*

> *"This woman became everything to me. Take her out of my life, and I don't know what I will do, how I will live, and whether I will survive at all. ..."*

"I know that if he leaves me, then all colors of life will be erased for me forever. From volumetric my life will become flat like photograph. ..."

At some point the following question usually really does pour over the head of a subject of manipulation like a bucket of cold water: "What will happen to me if one day the manipulator suddenly disappears from my life?" And, he/she realizes in horror that now life without a manipulator is not possible for him/her. Yes, he/she will probably survive, but it will no longer be life. After all, people quickly get used to good life.

With realization of this fact, at some point a subject of manipulation might panic. Covered with sticky sweat, terrified he/she goes through options in her/his head on how to ensure that a manipulator never leaves. And, despite the powerful stupor, in which the prospect of never again seeing a subject of his/her immeasurable admiration puts her, soon enough a subject of manipulation finds options for how to avoid this situation, how to keep the adored subject by his/her side. Probably for this reason every time a manipulator expresses some wish—a subject of manipulations rushes to fulfill it with incredible speed.

And, he/she is happy to do it. Why? Because a subject of manipulation perceives manipulator's wishes as a fortunate chance to please his/her deity, to do something pleasant for him/her, to show how much a manipulator is loved and appreciated and what he/she is ready to do for him. In the end, he/she is simply terrified of losing a manipulator.

People's incredible willpower and determination to get more and more "doses" of pleasure and happiness in the form of transmissions of personal suppression mode always amaze. Even a drug addict in need of another dose can hardly compete in intellectual creativity with a subject of manipulation, who does not want to lose a manipulator transmitting the suppression mode toward him/her.

*****

As mentioned above, from easygoing and quiet, a person toward whom a manipulator is transmitting his/her suppressing mode can turn into, as the saying goes, an explosive person if someone even tries, so to speak, "to look down his/her nose" at a subject of his/her burning adoration—a manipulator. And, if someone decides to criticize a manipulator or, even worse, to attack him, then the eyes of a subject of manipulation instantly fill with fury like in a bull and he/she literally begins to hurl thunderbolts.

It is not necessary to call upon a subject of manipulation to protect a person, who is transmitting the suppression mode toward him/her or to protect his/her relationship with a manipulator. At the mere hint of aggression toward a subject of his/her adoration, he/she begins to experience intense anger. Due to this anger, a subject of manipulation is ready to tear anyone, who attempts to encroach upon a manipulator to pieces.

In general, family, relatives, friends and former sexual partners of a subject of manipulation should forever forget that they once played some role in his/her life. Since if a subject of manipulation will be faced with a choice between them and a manipulator—he/she will sacrifice any one of them: his/her mother and father, best friend or even his/her child. For him/her, absolutely no one is more valuable than a person, who is transmitting the suppression mode toward him/her.

Also, it is strongly recommended to relatives and friends of a subject of manipulation not to try to convince him/her to change his/her mind about a manipulator and, even more so, to allow themselves to say something unpleasant about him or her. This can lead to a very, very tragic end.

> "I really didn't know that I am, as it appears, so hot-tempered. I began to notice that if someone even hints at any negativity toward Her, then like a wild gelding I immediately get upended and start to stamp hooves! I really become enraged. ..."

Here, we can add only that usually a subject of manipulation begins to "stamp his hooves" directly on the head of a poor critic or adviser. And, kinship does not play a role here because a manipulator, who applies a person's natural suppression mode to him/her, becomes the most important and the most valuable person than anyone else in the world for him/her.

> "Once my mother began to say something bad about her, I don't remember what exactly, but rage "hit me on the head" so hard that I lashed out at my mother almost with fists... It's a good thing that being a wise woman my mother did not insist, and so my anger quickly went away. ..."

> "I really got into a fight with my best friend, who allowed himself to say bad things about her. I was so angry that I think my friend was somewhat taken aback, he knows me since childhood. Now, I am afraid of myself. ..."

> "Once I had a fight with my sister, whom I love very much. It was so bad that it almost came to a physical fight. I don't know how I stopped myself, but I literally wanted to kill her when she said that

we are not a good pair. What saved my little sister was that what I felt intense anger I literally ran outside. If I wouldn't have done that, I really do not know how things would have ended. ..."

*****

Speaking of emotions: sooner or later, a person, toward whom someone regularly transmits his/her manipulation modes, begins to notice that he/she never experienced such rage, anger and aggression before. And, he/she is surprised with himself/herself. Moreover, he/she never allowed himself/herself to openly express these emotions before; especially toward people, who are close.

A subject manipulation is surprised to discover that at the mere hint of someone's dissatisfaction and aggression toward a manipulator he/she becomes as if a different person—absolutely fearless or, so to speak, "turretless." Before, other people probably succeeded in making him/her afraid and, so to speak, "putting in a stall" by rigorously shaking their index finger: "Stop acting so aggressively!" However, now everything is different. Inner strength that he/she never noticed before comes from the inside. And, this strength allows him/her to ignore anyone and anything.

A subject of manipulation becomes absolutely fearless when it is necessary, for example, to protect his/her deity (manipulator) from any attacks or when it is necessary to get hold of a manipulator or do something that he/she asked. However, this does not turn a subject of manipulation into an unbridled moron; on the contrary, his/her intellect becomes more powerful, more flexible, more creative. What gives him these strengths?

He/she gets such strength and might (psychical and through that—physical) from that ever since the time he/she met a manipulator—the life of a subject of manipulation became so joyful, so bright, so juicy in terms of energy that it literally saturates him/her with energy. For this reason, strength that he/she never experienced before awakes is a subject of manipulation and enables him/her to protect, stand up and fight for his/her happiness.

Happiness of a subject of manipulation is so great that like a huge charger it gives him/her enormous might, inspiration, enthusiasm. After some time, a person notices that his/her energy level raised and it seems that he/she is capable of moving mountains.

And, there is nothing surprising here. This is the result of applying individual manipulation modes to a person. Since, as mentioned above, manipulation   modes   are   that   what   is   required   for   human psychophysiology— they are "food," and in terms of energy gain this "food" is very high-calorie.

Joy, anticipation of a new meeting with a manipulator, and therefore a new dose of positivism—brings a person back to life; even from a state of deep depression. As a consequence of this awakened wild desire to live, many other desires, thoughts, ideas, aspiration to be active, to achieve something, to create something arise in a person. It is as if a powerful generator starts working inside him/her. Earth begins, so to speak, burning under his/her feet: what else to think of, what else to do?

This affect from application of natural manipulation modes was tested on clinical patients, suffering from severe depression and regularly taking powerful antidepressants. As a result, they forever parted with both pills and doctors.

*****

There is a saying—"life is in full swing." It seems quite relevant to use it in relation to a person, toward whom someone regularly transmits his natural manipulation modes; and, preferably all three of them: suppressing, balancing and stimulating.

Activeness, strong desire and appetite on all six factors (intellectual, physical, nutritional, emotional, sexual and environmental) flame up in a subject of manipulation. From gray or black and white his/her life becomes not just motley, colorful, but amazingly bright, and it is even possible to say sparkling, iridescent with new incredible colors and shades.

It is as if a person is reborn in this world. Richness of colors and savouriness of daily life become regular characteristics of his/her life. And, how much do you think any person is willing to pay for twenty four hours of pleasure and for his/her life to shine with bright colors once again? That is correct—he/she is ready to pay a lot. And, sometimes without regret he/she is ready to give everything to a person, who is transmitting his/her natural manipulation modes. And, as you can see, the reasons are worthwhile.

Each country has its own holiday or holidays, when every year people experience a big emotional lift. They await it, prepare for it with joy, etc. In Russia, this holiday is probably New Year, in the United States of America— Christmas and Independence Day. Now, imagine that a person, toward whom someone is transmitting his natural manipulation modes, is in this kind of a holiday mood every day: from early morning until night he/she is in an upbeat mood, feels positive, relaxed to the maximum, but at the same time feels inspired, lifted, ready to have unbridled fun, pleasure, communicate with other people, do something, run somewhere, and so on.

A person, toward whom someone is transmitting his/her manipulation modes, lives in these sensations; and not one day of a year, be an entire year. Now imagine that this, conditionally speaking, "Christmas story" does not end in February or May or even in September. Every day a person lives brightly, with pleasure, fun, taste and joy. Although even the most cheerful holiday, of course, is hopelessly dull in comparison with daily sensations of a subject of manipulation, who communicates with a manipulator.

*****

However, let's get back to the stimulation mode. Despite that during application of his personal suppression mode to a person, he/she experiences prevalence of sensations from the category of positive and pleasant—when a person learns this information about himself, at first he/she might feel upset.

This occurs because at some point a person finally realizes that it is very easy to discover all his/her "vulnerabilities;" and, what is even more unpleasant is that it is very easy to control him/her. And, of course, that he/she is absolutely defenseless against transmissions of his/her suppression mode (at least for a while) even if he/she knows his/her suppression mode. It is not pleasant to become aware of this. However, usually people deal with this on their own, alone and do not tell anyone about this.

However, when a person knows his/her manipulation modes and meets someone, who is trying to apply them in relation to him/her—he/she usually perceives this without fear and panic. Indeed, he/she no longer has to fear. People, who know, for example, their suppression mode, hardly ever will start to resist when someone transmits it. What is the point of resisting such pleasure? After all, you already know that your manipulation modes are very much necessary for your organism. And, you know that your suppression mode means a lot of extremely powerful sensations and experiences, which for the most part are incredibly pleasant. What is also important is that you already can (although with difficulty) resist a manipulator in cases when his/her requests do not coincide with your interests or threaten your well-being. At any time, like a fish you can get "off the hook," without forgetting to feast on tasty bait first. What to fear in this case?

A person, who knows his/her manipulation modes from the Catalog of Human Population, gains the ability to monitor and control a situation, in which someone is applying these modes in relation to him/her. Yes, he/she clearly knows what is happening. He/she clearly realizes that someone is trying to influence him/her using his/her suppression mode. He/she understands that inside himself/herself, in any case he/she will react to these attempts—this cannot be avoided because manipulation modes are part of the structure of human psyche. However, unlike a situation when a person is like a leaf being carried by a rapid stream—now, he/she can choose how to act.

Quite often, two people, who know each other's manipulation modes, begin to play out scenarios of their personal suppression modes to each other. Friends, relatives, spouses and sex partners can do this. Usually, the goal is not to make a person submit to you or force him to make some action that would benefit you. The goal is simply to have pleasure together, to do something nice for each other, to strengthen a relationship; and, of course, at the same time to strengthen skills—both as a manipulator and an object of manipulation.

In this situation, people often tend to make good-natured fun of each other. They say: "Thank you for my suppression mode, you pleased me." Or, "Don't you think it is time to stop stimulating me? I'm warning you, I'm about to give you a black eye!" And, they say this jokingly, without rancor, without getting offended at each other. On the contrary, they are grateful that another person paid attention, did a useful thing, fed an incredibly delicious and useful psychophysiological "food" in the form of natural manipulation modes. Positive feelings, which both people receive, get added up and, figuratively speaking, both invested a dollar and both got two dollars. Plus, their connection, their relationship eventually becomes strong like armor and any external power can no longer break this relationship.

And, from the point of view of a manipulator—knowledge, application of manipulation modes of another person is always highly effective in terms of getting results. As a nice addition to this, manipulation eventually turns into a fascinating process that is built on playing as a principle; it turns out that manipulation is a game, but with serious results.

However, we think that the main thing in this game is not to get into the role of "ruler of destinies" too much and to perceive a subject of manipulation humanely, in a humane way, knowing that you have a serious tool, which is like a knife that can be used to spread butter on bread, but also can be used to kill. Unfortunately, as many years of our practice have shown, people sometimes forget about this.

¹ By "natural images" we do not mean some natural images selected randomly—we mean specific natural images, as images, by which individual manipulation modes of a subject of manipulation are recorded in his unconscious.

² However, only if he/she knows his/her suppression mode. If a subject of manipulation does not know his/her natural control modes, then return to reality is not possible while influencing continues. Even when transmissions of suppression mode already stopped, for some time (for quite a while, actually) a subject of manipulation continues to remain "out of reality," his/her consciousness is clouded, intellect does not work, and so on.

³ Unlike modern psychologists, we prefer information from ancient sources, which states that a human has only five emotions; no more and no less.

CHAPTER 5

PROCESS AND RESULTS OF CONTROLLING *HOMO SAPIENS* ON THE BASIS OF ARTIFICIAL IMAGES

Now, consider results of attempts to control a human by using artificial images.

In this case, there is no single method. All methods in this category are the same only in one thing—a manipulator plays a role that is based on an artificial image (images), which is made up by someone or by him and has no relation to the instinctive sphere of a subject of manipulation. While in the previous chapter we described influence on psyche of *Homo sapiens* on the basis of knowledge of specific images of individual sphere of unconscious of a subject of manipulation.

To describe the process of control of *Homo sapiens* using artificial images, as an example, we chose women's attempts to manipulate men[1]. After all, by nature the desire for power is stronger in women, and especially for power over representatives of the opposite sex—consciously or unconsciously. We will not explain in this book why this is so, as it is already described in detail in a book titled *Women's Thirst For Power Over Men Is The Pathway To Become A Garbage* (by A. Davydov and O. Skorbatyuk).

*****

However, first we will provide a brief clarification.

All women without exception are big fans of manipulating other people (of both genders). As we found out, this happens because reception of power over someone automatically turns on sensations of happiness, euphoria in women. However, men are more preferable as subjects of manipulation because in this case the "defeated" not only gives the above-mentioned "high" to his "victress," but often also spends his money on her (it does not matter whether he spends a lot of money or not—this depends on a woman's luck).

Usually, a woman's point of view is that if she is successful in manipulation of a man, then she does not need to work hard in order to have a high social status, fame, prominence; there is no need "to get to the top," to make money, and to fight for all this—a man will do all this for her. She only needs to correctly "motivate" a man to achievements by manipulating his psyche and body. After all, from a woman's point of view a man is just a resource; although a very diverse resource, from which this and that can be obtained[2].

While a "conquered" man strains, breaks through, "suffers from throes of creation," fights for money, power, social benefits and so on, a woman can look through glossy magazines, go to a hair salon, a sauna, visit a cosmetologist or get a massage, get some rest, breathe some fresh air and admire nature's beauty, chat with a girlfriend or with her mother, do her nails, watch television, lie on a couch, or visit a gym "to twist her booty" and flirt with other men. After all, no matter what stories women tell about remaining faithful, they tend to always seek to have, so to speak, "an alternate airfield" in case a used resource becomes exhausted or "closes down."

And, if a woman becomes tired of openly lounging around while a man engages in business and makes money, then she can play a game called "I'm working." When a woman has a man-breadwinner, she goes to work not because of the need to earn her daily bread, but because she has nothing to do and she is very bored. And, also because she already, so to speak, "hilled up" all men at a gym and needs new subjects to flirt with and not only that. After all, in this civilization women work and "do business," figuratively speaking, between pads and condoms.

There is also a category of women (and there are many women from this category), who have children in order to sit at home, do what they want, not worry about money and always have a possibility to manipulate a man. And, it does not matter with what all this gets decorated.

However, once a woman has power, she is forced to constantly worry about not losing it. As a result, the entire life of any woman becomes one big fight for power. However, this is not the worst thing. The worst thing is that in this fight for power a woman is quickly degrades and gets terribly worn out. Despite modern cosmetic and other tricks, she begins to get sick, age and lose "marketability."

We found out the cause of premature and very rapid aging of women in this civilization. The cause is not in biological processes. Onset of aging at forty years of age (and sometimes earlier) is not a natural process. Very specific mechanisms turn on the program of aging early. Which ones exactly? Artificial images, which women actively use to manipulate men.

However, we got a bit off topic. We are offering you to take a look not only from the side, but also from the inside at how the process of manipulation using artificial images occurs when done by a woman.

*****

If a woman did not find herself in a mirror in the morning, then this means that today it is necessary for her to get into some character, to play some role in order to influence someone. Within a very short time, a woman writes a scenario for herself in her mind, chooses a role, costume, make-up. And, she does all this literally between toilet paper, a toothbrush, soap and a towel. Oh, if masters of the art of acting knew this—they would just weep!

This task is not simple because a woman needs to first find the right image or images to solve a current task or tasks, and then she needs to become an actress and embody them (act them out). Often she has to play not just one role a day because sometimes there are more than one or two people, from whom a woman needs something (among family, at work, among friends). Since the main subjects of women's interest in terms of manipulation are men—this category includes a husband, a son, a father, a brother, a boss, male colleagues, male friends, and lovers.

After all, a woman wants to get something from each one—both material and nonmaterial; for example: attention, compliments, interest (including sexual), sex, care, respect, help, etc. However, of course, the most important thing for a woman is to get the above-mentioned "high" from manipulation—a sensation of happiness and euphoria from controlling a man's soul.

However, the trouble is that images, by which a woman can manipulate others, are different in different situations. In order to seduce a man it is necessary to use one image, a completely different image is needed in order to make a man pity her or help her, and another image to ensure that he sees her as an excellent housewife and mother. And so on. After all, the image of "femme fatale," an insidious seductress is not appropriate when you wish to show your husband what an exemplary mother you are and get corresponding benefits from this.

There are many artificial images made up to help a woman in this and thanks to men they can always be borrowed from literature, movies, and other sources of so-called "culture." However, first it is necessary to arrange each of these images for yourself in order to act them out. Also, as it was stated above, it is impossible to achieve different goals using the same artificial image. And, this is a problem.

Plus, a woman has to be a director and an actress at the same time and this takes a lot of energy. It is probably impossible to find a professional actor, who spends all day on stage without weekends, holidays, lunch breaks, and in addition plays not one role, but several at the same time. Women do this and for this reason they "go out of circulation" so early.

For example, consider women, who are over fifty years old. Most men of the same age are still, as they say, "in business": they work, support a family, have young lovers (plus, support them), have hobbies, and sometimes even have enough energy for a creative process. While a woman has enough only for manipulation games, which she plays in between pills and visits to doctors and cosmetologists; but, what to do—she got worn out.

Therefore, at some point a man leaves his "old nag" and turns to young women, who have not yet worn themselves out too much by their acting. Meanwhile, a woman racks her brains: "Why is he like this with me? I gave him all my life!" And, indeed, she really gave.

However, to no avail.

*****

Now, let's get back to description of the process of controlling a man using artificial images. In order to find an appropriate image to impersonate and to use for achievement of some goal by the means of manipulation, a woman, so to speak, "falls deep within herself." When she does this, she is convinced that she will find a solution in the process of her intellectual activity. In vain! The space, into which a woman falls in such cases, is neither her intellect nor she herself. This space is an archive of "files" with recordings of "priceless collection" called "Ahnenerbe"[3].

Intellect of a person, who does not know his/her natural program, is completely blocked by artificial "software." It disguises itself as so-called "inner voice," and tells a person what to do in a particular situation and how he/she should live in general. Women are no exception. On the contrary, they definitely can be considered fanatical guardians of Ahnenerbe. After all, women, mothers input this virus into their children, and thus pass it on from generation to generation.

However, we got a bit sidetracked. So, as it seems to her, a woman is thinking, but in reality she is frantically looking for the necessary "file" in her personal "treasure of wisdom," heritage left by parents (upbringers): this is how her mother acted in such situations, and this is how her grandmother acted, and these were the steps taken by her big sister, aunt, etc.

Behind each behavioral scenario from this "treasury" are artificial images, those cultural archetypes (although this has nothing to do with true culture), which a mother or a grandmother used as the basis of their behavior at some point; for example: artistic images of characters from movies, romance novels and other books, from songs and other types of "folk art."

And, all would be fine and dandy, but grandmother's or mother's recipes, which, figuratively speaking, are moth-eaten, reeking of mothballs no longer work: thirty, forty, fifty or more years passed since their creation— times changed and men changed. However, in order to understand this, a woman will have to go through a failure or a series of failures trying to manipulate men with the help of mother's-grandmother's recipes.

So, a woman turns to modern sources for another recipe on how to manipulate men (what images, what roles to play for them). Sources, from which this "white sheep" "drinks," are low grade: women's novels, television, movies, glossy magazines, the Internet (which has long been turned into informational scrapyard), girlfriends (who are just as "wise" as she is herself) and "experts"-psychologists, who do not know anything about human soul (psyche) and its structure. In general, there are not too many choices. However, another thing is worse: manipulation tricks offered by these sources have long been fully known to men, they are extremely primitive models and standards from the category "one for all." It is always like this and only like this in the case of methods of control of a person on the basis of artificial images.

Finally, having found a more or less suitable image for realization, all that a woman has to do is use the recipe. Note that this is not her recipe—it is someone else's. As mentioned above, this recipe can be fresh, for example, from some magazine article a la "How to get and keep a man" or it can be covered with moss and a layer of dust—from her grandmother. However, since a woman has long forgotten about her grandmother and about advices from a psychological article that she recently read, she is fully convinced that a recipe for how to manipulate a man is her own creation.

While the whole "creation" is only in that a woman chose several artificial images and made a kind of "collage" from them: hairdo from this one, a dress from that one, and voice and behavior from another one. She does not want to copy some actress from a movie or a character from a book exactly—what about, as they say, individuality? Despite that a woman did not come up with anything herself (because she is simply incapable of it), this way she gets a pleasant sensation that she is the author of this "bright image." And, she is proud that, as it seems to her, she found a solution herself and, supposedly, kept her individuality (even though she did not have and does not have individuality).

This "collage" or rather a peculiar "Frankenstein" (which, by the way, is just as monstrous) assembled from different parts like a transformer—becomes a scenario for a woman-manipulator, which tells her how to look, sound, smell, move, speak, express emotions (which, by the way, she really does not feel on the inside since she turned herself into a real log a long time ago), and so on. A woman uses such a "Frankenstein" as the basis of her behavior in the process of manipulation of a man and proceeds to conquer the next "Everest" named Joe, Don or John.

And, note that a woman never knows in advance whether or not she will conquer this "Everest."

*****

Once she parts with a bath-room, where she created another "masterpiece"-"Frankenstein," with dazzling speed a woman begins to transform: makeup, hairdo, clothes and accessories, facial expression, posture, fragrances, etc. And then, she presents herself to a subject of manipulation in all her glory. As it seems to her, she is simply charming and everyone simply must be crazy about her.

What about reality? In reality, a man for whom a woman makes this "performance" has his own idea of what a woman worthy of his attention must be like. Moreover, these preferences are built into his unconscious since birth as images of his suppression mode, which was discussed in the previous chapter.

His own, individual cliché called "The Woman of My Dreams" is implanted in the unconscious of each man: the way she looks, how she dresses, speaks, moves, what she eats, and so on. As already mentioned, there are two hundred and ninety three subtypes of biological type *Homo sapiens* and, of course, each one has their own "Dream-Woman," the only one, and they do not need any other. For this reason, in ninety nine percent out of one hundred, a woman-manipulator with a scenario from her grandmother or from cheap literature does not fit the expected "type."

The most that "a great woman-manipulator" can get from a man is some of his attention toward her. After all, people are civilized. However, no one can forbid a man from forming an opinion in his mind about a woman-manipulator in the range from "Well, each woman has her own cockroaches in her head" to "What a stupid woman!" (it all depends on the level of his intelligence). And, all this happens only because a woman does not know a man's suppression mode. Therefore, she does not know and cannot know on the basis of which images (natural, not artificial) this man becomes interested, impressed, excited, seduced, conquered, and controlled.

When acting out her "brilliant manipulation scenario," women's intuition usually hints at that something is going wrong in the course of her performance. Yes, a man shows her signs of attention, smiles, and even flirts with her, but... And then, a woman urgently selects and embodies a different "stage image" from another, for example, cheap romance novel; then another one, and another one. In this sense, a woman acts like a burglar with a bunch of keys, which she inserts into a lock hoping that one of them will suddenly open a door.

Once a woman understands that she cannot find a key to this outlandish lock named Michael or Robert (and, it really is quite impossible to do by guessing), she starts using the most primitive methods of conquering men: "bow lips," batting her eyes, licking her lips, displaying different body parts and other vulgar tricks from cheap porn, which raise at least some interest in men toward women, at least at the level of a reflex.

Watching all this, a man can only conclude that in front of him is an ordinary whore. A man says to himself: "Well, since she wants me so much, why not." And, like a true knight, who supposedly goes on a leash of "women's tricks," he throws her on a bed (at best, and at worse—simply leans her against a wall facing away from him in a corresponding position).

Moreover, usually a man does "it" without washing his hands and private parts, even though he sat in an office all day, as well as in the car, and probably went to the bathroom multiple times with different purposes. This occurs at least because in his eyes a woman-manipulator automatically gets the label "whore" after all her "secret tricks," with all the consequences and specific attitude toward her.

And, while a woman is "resting her soul" from directing-acting hardships and is absorbed by "The Man of Her Dreams" in her fantasies (whom women usually imagine in the place of their sexual partners), essentially a man also is having sex not with her, but with "The Woman of His Dreams" in his fantasies, putting his dirty hands and other body parts wherever he pleases. It is not surprising that women often have to take pills from various infections and other diseases, and visit gynecologists so often.

*****

So, all that a woman achieved with her "manipulation" was that she got used like a free whore. Although it is very likely that sex with this man was not her goal. Possibly, what she wanted from him was to get a promotion, financial assistance, a gift, participation in some of her affairs, or simply that what women call "love." However, she does not get all this from a man, and even if she manages to get some of what she really wanted—she never gets it fully and it is always not all that she wanted.

Absolutely all women, who use artificial images to influence psyche of a man, are well familiar with such a result. Even the most talented women-manipulators never get exactly that what they expect to get as a result of manipulation and never to the full extent. Hence, a typical woman's conclusion: "All men are pigs." Although what do pigs have to do with men, if the issue is in women themselves and those "brilliant" manipulation scenarios (meaning—images since an image is the basis of any scenario), which they use?

We will not go deeper into the jungle called "a man – a woman – an image" in this book. We will just say that it only seems to women that they themselves invent images, which they use to manipulate men. In reality, these images are invented by... men. However, those people, who are interested, can read about this in the first two books of the series titled A Log With Legs Spread Wide (by A. Davydov, O. Skorbatyuk). The first book is titled How Men Turn Women Into Nothing and the second is titled How Goddesses Are Turned Into Logs: World History Of Turning Women Into Mats.

*****

After another "director's-actor's" failure, women are usually very tired, in a terrible mood, full of hate and wild anger, have a lousy sense of self, and experience a desperate desire to take revenge on all "these pigs" sometime in the future. It has long been known what such emotional states do to human body—like hydrochloric acid, they corrode him/her away from the inside. This means that a manipulator's nails will start breaking, hair will start falling out, more wrinkles will appear on the skin, and so on.

This means that a woman will "suddenly" get a headache or stomachache, will start vomiting, etc. It is also possible that because of this she will overdo it with alcohol or will "eat something to relieve stress" and add some extra pounds to her figure, which is already far from ideal. And, this is the best case scenario. Either way, a woman already paid for controlling using artificial images with part of her health and life. And, unfortunately, this is not the "final payment."

However, more importantly, what is the result? Firstly, there is absence of the needed result from influence on a man, for whom she made her performance. Secondly, now she is in a position of a fool and/or a whore in the eyes of a man (as well as in his own eyes). Thirdly, she got health issues (now or in the near future). And, this is not the worst thing that happens to a manipulator, who uses artificial images. The following is much worse than this.

*****

It was found that a human cell "sees" images. And, it unconditionally embodies an image that a host or a hostess "throws" it. When it "sees" an image, a cell embodies it at the level of physiology (just as unquestioningly as a sergeant in an army). In other words, if a "Frankenstein" was shown to a cell of a woman's body, then sooner or later a woman will see a monster in a mirror in front of her. And, by the age of forty-fifty, she is guaranteed to see the difference between how she looked when she was twenty years old and how she looks now, and the difference will be in favor of "Frankenstein."

The thing is that functions of a cell do not include discussion about what is beneficial for a person and what is not. A cell is a soldier that simply follows orders of an Image-general and does it without hesitation, precisely and on time. However, a woman does not even suspect that this mechanism exists.

Here are some other examples. Based on what was stated above, probably it is not difficult to guess what will happen if in her attempts to manipulate (men as well) a woman will decide to embody images like "I'm weak and defenseless" or "I'm a so stupid" or "I'm white and fluffy." In this context, it does not matter whether a man will believe in this acting or not and what a woman will get from him. What is more important is that specific messages get sent to her cells: become weak, become defenseless, become stupid, become white, become fluffy. And, cells of her organism consider all of these commands as calls to action.

And, rest assured that very soon cells of a woman's body will turn her into a weak, sick, helpless being, a complete idiot and an old woman. A woman certainly will not understand what happened since women know about images and their influence on human psychophysiology even less than men know about it. However, a woman really will feel ill and weak, her intellect will work worse and worse and she will begin to see signs of physiological aging in a mirror in front of her.

Why are we talking about aging in this case? Because mostly old women are white, weak and helpless. Consequently, the process of turning on mechanisms of aging in a woman's organism is guaranteed. Cells also do not have a problem with embodiment of fluffiness—a woman will have to buy lots of razors, depilatory creams and tweezers to remove hair above the upper lip and other places.

Or consider, for example, a Barbie doll—an image that is well known and loved by generations of many women[4]. When a cell sees this image, it turns a girl into a stupid log, which feels nothing, wants nothing, and which begins to move and to live only as a result of some influences from the outside: something happens, someone wants or demands something from her, someone offers something to her, she needs to carry out some actions or she will be in trouble, and so on. For more information about the image of a Barbie doll and the consequences of that girls play with these dolls can be found in the book titled A Barbie Doll Is A Serial Killer (by A. Davydov, O. Skorbatyuk, K. Bazilevsky).

Here is another example. A woman often wishes that a man would always be near her. What are the dangers of this? The danger here is that sooner or later a terrible, incurable disease, a hospital bed or intensive care are guaranteed for her. Why? Because only in this case there is a guarantee that she will get a man, who will sit by her side. However, with a high probability this will not be a man, whom she wanted to see next to her—instead it will be a doctor or a nurse.

It does not matter to cells of a human organism, orders of which images to execute—natural or artificial. A cell does not know that artificial images are very harmful for human psychophysiology. A cell does not know that natural images give life and that artificial images lead to death. By nature a cell is not designed to think; in addition to everything else, it has a completely different function—to execute orders implanted in a particular image. And, rest assured that a cell will execute each of these orders precisely and on time. A human is the one who must think. And, it does not matter with which sexual characteristics he was born—male or female.

If after everything that was stated above a reader will decide that it makes sense to continue to use this type of control of a human—now you know that for using artificial images to manipulate (no matter whom and with what goal), you will pay with your skin, hair, nails, lungs, heart, stomach, genitals, intestines, liver, and so on. In short, you will pay with your health, your youth, your life.

Those people, who think this price is too high, now know that today it is not a problem to find out your personal natural images and images of manipulation modes of people you are interested from the Catalog of Human Population. If we consider this in the context of a saying "to kill two birds with one stone," then by finding out your own and other people's natural images from this Catalog—you are guaranteed to save your health and can manipulate others in any way you want.

*****

It should also be noted that even though this example was about women, information about the influence of artificial images on human psychophysiology equally applies to men. Therefore, playing with artificial images is not recommended for men either.

As for men's attempts to manipulate people—it does not make sense to describe them in this book because essentially they do not differ from women's attempts; the principle is the same—"a shot in the dark." The only difference is that instead of a white-fluffy-helpless Barbie, a man uses a male etalon-"Frankenstein," for example, a brave-courageous-resolute Superman-Bond-Batman-Tarzan. That is all. There is a lot of material for creation of such a "Frankenstein" for men in this civilization, for any taste.

Plus, considering that for some reason every man in this civilization thinks that he is like the Creator and tries to create his own artificial images (for women (as it is described in our books titled How Men Turn Women Into Nothing and How Goddesses Are Turned Into Logs—World History Of Turning Women Into Mats), as well as for themselves), a man "can come up with" something else to add to his "Frankenstein." However, such "creativity" does not make men more successful manipulators when compared to women.

It is simply boring to discuss manipulation by men on the basis of artificial images that they created themselves or borrowed from society. This process does not deserve attention because men's attempts to manipulate someone on this basis are just as funny, naïve, primitive and just as "successful" as women's. Proof of this is obvious—there are few successful (meaning—rich, influential) men. The majority of them are forced to work for someone else their entire lives and that is all. They achieve things only by their work, "blood and sweat" and are incapable of achieving anything by any other means and are incapable of achieving anything else.

Men in this civilization are also "being had" easily and regularly, just like a woman-manipulator in the example above (in the sexual sense as well). While men consider themselves practically deities compared to "the silly chickens"—in reality women regularly use men as a resource. For example, for more than one millennium women send men like miners "to work" and quite successfully live at their expense (when they set this goal for themselves) regardless of that women are not professionals in manipulation.

*****

In conclusion of the topic of artificial images we must disappoint you. Life on artificial "software" does not free a *Homo sapiens* of any gender from automatic (at the level of a reflex) obedience of his/her natural manipulation modes.

It is much easier to uncover artificial "software" in contrast to natural "software" that is described in Shan Hai Jing. Hence the possibility to legalize any "secrets" and "mysteries" of a person, who lives on the basis of artificial images, and we demonstrate this in many of our books and articles. None of you will be able to protect your "hidden treasures of the soul." After all, consciousness (awareness[5]) is that what you do not possess.

Now, we suppose it is time to move on to checking how the natural tool for controlling a human—manipulation modes—work on practice. However, first please read brief instructions on how to do it correctly. These instructions are provided in the next part of this book.

[1] By women we mean all women (of any race, nationality, cultural background, ages, social strata) because all women (and men) live in a civilization where artificial images are used instead of natural images—used as both "software" of *Homo sapiens* and a tool to manage/control a human.

[2] More information about the true essence of a being called "woman" and relationships between women and men is available in book series titled A Log With Legs Spread Wide.

[3] A reader can find out what this is from the first book in the Catalog of Human Souls series titled *Homo Sapiens* Are Bio-Robots. Human "Software" (by O. Skorbatyuk, K. Bazilevsky). See Part 3 titled Ahnenerbe: Your Killer Is Under Your Skin (by A. Davydov, O. Skorbatyuk).

[4] A Barbie (from Barbara) is a toy, mostly for girls between three and fourteen years old. It was launched in 1959 in the USA (in the state of Wisconsin). Barbie's creator is Ruth Handler. She was the wife of Elliot Handler, who founded Mattel, Inc.

[5] According to our research, words "awareness", "consciously", "with awareness" mean a person's ability to monitor images, based on which he/she lives.

PART 3

PRACTICAL PART:
APPLYING MANIPULATION
MODES OF *HOMO SAPIENS*

Sketch © 2000 Andrey Davydov

CHAPTER 1

HOW TO TEST THE TOOL CALLED SUPPRESSION MODE

In the next chapter of this book we provided a suppression mode scenario of one of two hundred and ninety three subtypes of *Homo sapiens*; dates of birth of people, who belong to this subtype, are October 12th of leap years and October 13th of common years.

Their age, gender, race, nationality, place of residence and social status do not matter. These are people, on whom we are offering you to test the work of natural manipulation modes of *Homo sapiens*, which were found in Shan Hai Jing by researcher Andrey Davydov, in order to make sure that the Catalog of Human Population really exists and that any person can use it in his/her daily life right now.

*****

We think that in order to do this test it will not be a problem for anyone to find men and women, who were born on October 12th of leap years and/or October 13th of common years. If it so happens that you do not find these people in your circles, we think that finding them elsewhere will not be a problem in the age of the Internet. You can always find people with the needed date of birth online and communicate with them [1].

Do not think that if you found a person, who was born on October 12th of leap years or October 13th of common years in your circles—it is the only person, on whom you can test how the suppression mode provided in this book works. On planet Earth, a huge number of people were born on the same day and, according to information from the ancient source Shan Hai Jing (which turned out to be the Catalog of Human Population), all of them have the same[2] natural "software": the same program and the same manipulation modes. In scientific terms—all of them belong to one human subtype.

So do not limit yourself when testing the suppression mode of people, who were born on October 12th of leap years and October 13th of common years to only one person. It is not without reason that in science any theory is tested on a large number of test subjects (thousands); only this process is called "verification"[3]. Anyway, why limit yourself to manipulation of one person, if today there are over twenty million people in the world, who are exactly the same as he/she is?

When testing how manipulation modes of *Homo sapiens* work, we recommend that you do not avoid contact with people born on October 12th of leap years or October 13th of common years, with whom you have never communicated before. At least because the process of applying natural manipulation modes with people you do not know very well is usually easier.

Why? The thing is that people, who have known you for some time, have already formed an image of you inside them. Therefore, when they see you acting out their suppression mode in a new hypostasis, they can get a bit surprised and stunned by the change in your self-presentation and behavior: "You are somehow different today, unusual." Why spend time on explanations? Would it not be easier to try out a new tool called manipulation modes of a human on your new acquaintances as well?

Of course, it is also not a problem if you have known a subject of manipulation for a long time because anyway he/she will not be able to resist transmissions of manipulation modes. It is just that in this case the process of obtaining results can be somewhat delayed because a subject of manipulation will have to get used to your new "image."

However, this will not continue for too long because your new "image" from the suppression mode is guaranteed to fit the taste of a subject of manipulation. As a result, he/she will give up quickly and will be happy to see "another person" in you. He/she will explain this to himself/herself by that you, for example, "finally came to your senses," listened to his/her opinions, requests, wishes. Those people, who do not know about the Catalog of Human Population and that two hundred and ninety three different human subtypes exist in nature, tend to consider their own lifestyle, habits, qualities of character the best, the most correct, etalon.

And, they are convinced that everyone must live in the same way as they do and this is just what they seek in other people. So, just let them, as this makes the process of manipulation easier—every person has the right to live in illusions, but every person also has the right to use this.

Also, we remind you that nationality, race, place of birth and residence do not play any role in application of natural manipulation modes of *Homo sapiens*. These are only correctors, which to not fundamentally change the subtype program of a human. Therefore, you can use the same suppression mode (and any other mode) with a person of any skin color, etc. Age, gender, social status, etc. also do not play any role. Manipulation modes of *Homo sapiens* work on any representative of the biological type "human;" hence they are so valuable.

Therefore, you can apply the suppression mode provided in Chapter 2 to any person, who was born on October 12th of leap years or October 13th of common years: no matter if it is a man, a woman, a member of your family, your friend, your boss, an elderly person or a child.

We also remind you that manipulation modes (as well as all other information from the Catalog of Human Population) are applicable not only in the sphere of interpersonal relations and not only in everyday problems. The Catalog of Human Population as a whole and manipulation modes of *Homo sapiens* in particular are successfully applied in all spheres of human activity: from so-called "fights in the kitchen" to the top political level.

*****

However, before you start experimenting, please make sure that people you chose really are suitable for this test. First of all, make sure that you know the exact year of birth of a person, to whom you decided to play the role from his/her suppression mode. Secondly, make sure that you checked whether it is a leap year or a common year. It does not make sense to start testing without taking these steps first. And, here is why.

If it turns out that one of the people you found was born on October 12th of a common year or on October 13th of a leap year, then this person is absolutely not suitable for testing. Since he/she is a representative of another subtype of *Homo sapiens* and has completely different manipulation modes (including suppression mode). Be warned that simple lack of attention can seriously distort the results of your testing.

People born on October 12th of common years and October 13th of leap years have absolutely nothing in common with representatives of the subtype, to which people born on October 12th of leap years and October 13th of common years belong. They are representatives of other subtypes and have completely different qualities, properties and functions; and, what is most important in this context is that they have different manipulation modes.

Therefore, you will not be able to get anything from them by using the suppression mode of people, who were born on October 12th of leap years and October 13th of common years. They simply will not react to this mode.

Of course, coincidences happen because the Catalog of Human Population contains two hundred and ninety three descriptions of human subtypes, while there are three hundred and sixty five days of a year. However, in order to use this information it is necessary to know exactly which human programs reproduce a few consecutive days. You do not have this information and it is impossible to guess or uncover this without the Catalog of Human Population. So, do not waste your time.

How to determine if some year is a leap year or a common year? Here is list, based on which you can tell. This list contains only leap years.

Complete list of leap years of XX and XXI centuries:

1904, 1908, 1912, 1916, 1920, 1924, 1928, 1932, 1936, 1940, 1944, 1948, 1952, 1956, 1960, 1964, 1968, 1972, 1976, 1980, 1984, 1988, 1992, 1996, 2000, 2004, 2008, 2012, 2016, 2020, 2024, 2028, 2032, 2036, 2040, 2044, 2048, 2052, 2056, 2060, 2064, 2068, 2072, 2076, 2080, 2084, 2088, 2092, 2096.

We recommend being especially careful when it comes to women because at a certain age they tend to disinform others about their year of birth in order to seem younger. In this case, it is probably better to refer to official sources, where the date of birth of a woman is stated (her passport, her driver's license, public records).

Also, prior to working with the suppression mode scenario of people born on October 12th of leap years and October 13th of common years, a manipulator should set a goal or goals. Do you simply want to see how someone born on one of these dates will react to his/her suppression mode? Of course, this is wonderful, but we would recommend to a least set a simple objective for yourself—to get something from a subject of manipulation.

It can be something insignificant, but it is better than manipulation that is not goal-oriented. And, here is why. Not all of you are professional psychologists, who are able to properly monitor and understand reactions of other people. Therefore, you might not notice reactions to the suppression mode or you might interpret them incorrectly. For this reason, some specific things will be the best criterion for presence or absence of a result from manipulation.

For example, if it is not your first day of communication with a person, who was born on October 12th of leap years or October 13th of common years, you can try to get from that person something that you could not manage to get before (something material or not—it does not matter). This will be much more indicative than simply your opinion about reactions of a particular person. However, please be realistic and do not make plans to get a boat as a gift right away. Why this is so is described in Part 3 Chapter 3 of this book.

*****

Now, we will briefly describe how to use the scenario of the suppression mode provided in the following chapter with real people, who were born on October 12th of leap years or October 13th of common years.

Once you are sure that people you found really were born on October 12th of leap years or October 13th of common years, proceed to carefully reading the scenario of their suppression mode, which we provided in the following chapter of this book.

First, the scenario includes a brief general description⁴ of basic character traits of a person, who a manipulator needs to play. This part of the manipulation scenario will help a manipulator "feel the role," as the actors say—"get into character"⁵.

However, the role that a manipulator has to play in order for a subject of manipulation to submit to him does not end with a general description. After it, you will see in the scenario a description on six factors: intellectual, physical, nutritional, emotional, sexual and environmental⁶. A manipulator needs to act out all this as well to a person he/she wants to subdue.

When possible, it is better to act out all six factors, as in this case manipulation is always more effective. However, if a manipulator is not planning to have sexual relations with a subject of manipulation, then part of the sexual factor can be skipped—in this case a manipulator should use only information about the attitude of a person to family, parents, children (if this information is provided in a scenario).

How to use information from six factors provided in a manipulation scenario? Here is an example from the nutritional factor. Each time when a manipulator has meals together with a subject of manipulation (no matter where: at home, at a restaurant, at a party, etc.), he/she needs to demonstrate eating habits from the nutritional factors of the suppression mode. For example, the following is stated in the suppression mode scenario of people born on October 12th of leap years and October 13th of common years: "loves to eat small fish" and "prefers to add ginger to dishes." This means that a manipulator must consume these products, when communicating with a subject of manipulation.

The same goes for the rest of the factors. If it is stated in the scenario that this person "always has red clothing items in a wardrobe"—it means that a manipulator needs to wear red clothes, accessories, and so on. More information on how to act out manipulation modes can be found on our website under Frequently Asked Questions (section titled Questions Related

To Using Information From The Catalog Of Human Population On Practice)   -   http://www.humanpopulationacademy.org/faq-category/questions-related-to-using-information-from-the-catalog-of-human-population-on-practice/.

We remind you that if you do not possess something that needs to be demonstrated (whether it is personal qualities, material assets, etc.), then you can simply declare it using words. For example, you can state that you own (or owned in the past) a certain type of housing, jewelry, etc. and that you once had a profession, family, parents, children, hobbies from the suppression mode of a subject of manipulation.

*****

It is necessary to play the character described in the suppression mode scenario like an actor plays a role in theater or film. And, you must play this role every time you communicate with a subject of manipulation. This is extremely important. Why? This question will be answered below.

This role should be acted out as precisely as possible; that is, without inclusion of your personal qualities, preferences, life algorithms, and so on. Keep in mind that you are not the one described in the suppression mode scenario of people born on October 12th of leap years and October 13th of common years, even if some of the qualities of this character apply to you personally as well.

If you want to see with your own eyes how people, who were born on October 12th of leap years and October 13th of common years, will react to their suppression mode—do not arrange/modify the manipulation scenario. When acting out any manipulation scenario—you cannot act based on "I think it will be much better and more correct to do it like this" or "Why not also do this?" Etc. Do not add your vision, your speculations, your preferences, etc. to the role described in the manipulation scenario because if you do—the scenario simply will not work.

It is not recommended to even approach acting out any manipulation scenario (not only the suppression mode scenario of people born on October 12th of leap years and October 13th of common years) according to the principle "this is comfortable/not comfortable for me (I like this/I do not like this, I want to do it like this/I do not want to do it like this)." Do not change the scenario to "fit you." This is extremely unproductive. If in manipulation of another person you behave not in the way that you should, but in a way that you want/like (or in a way that is convenient for you), then do not expect results. After all, in this case you are working not toward a result, but toward satisfaction of your "I want", "I like", "comfortable for me."

In summary, a manipulator should put all of his/her personal qualities, wishes, desires, preferences, opinions in, so to speak, the farthest corner possible until the end of communication/meeting with a subject of manipulation. Since when you are playing a role from someone's natural manipulation mode—you transform, become a different person for this entire time. And, specifically due to this a subject of manipulation begins to obey you.

It is necessary to keep in mind that a subject of manipulation can start to obey you ONLY because at some point he/she will believe that you really are the person from his/her natural suppression mode. There are simply no other reasons for this. Therefore, if you suddenly start to deviate from the role described in the manipulation scenario (no matter for what reason)— this will make a subject of manipulation doubt that you are the person, who you claim to be. As a result, he/she will, as fishermen say, "get off the hook" and you will be left, figuratively speaking, "without a catch."

*****

Now, we will briefly describe the main principles of acting out the suppression mode of people, who were born on October 12th of leap years or October 13th of common years[7].

First of all, it is necessary not only to read the scenario, comprehend it, and "try on the role," but also it is desirable to memorize this role. After all, actors always know roles they play by heart. An actor cannot allow himself to go on stage until he learns a role. The situation is analogous with manipulation scenarios.

The better you know the role from the suppression mode of a person, the easier and, most importantly, the more effective (in terms of results) you will act out this role for him/her. And, if you are only partially familiar with the role from the manipulation mode, then there is always a risk that you will forget, confuse or distort something and will transmit a mode with mistakes, incorrectly. Then, do not be surprised when a subject of manipulation will, figuratively speaking, tell you like Stanislavsky[8]: "I do not believe you!"[9] For you, as a manipulator, this will mean a complete failure and lack of results from your work.

Once you learn the role, you can begin to act it out for a subject of manipulation. The key moment in acting out manipulation modes (just as in any theater and film productions) is transformation. For those people, who are not familiar with the art of acting, we recommended to at least familiarize yourselves with the system created by Stanislavsky, which is mentioned above.

In a nutshell, Stanislavsky's System is a theory of performing arts, the method of acting technique. In this system, the problem of conscious comprehension of the creative process of creation of a role is solved for the first time and ways of getting into an image (transformation) get determined. The goal is to achieve complete psychological authenticity of acting.

World-famous actors, supporters of the Stanislavsky's System are: Marilyn Monroe, Charles Spencer Chaplin, Marlon Brando, Robert De Niro, Al Pacino, Meryl Streep, Anthony Hopkins, Johnny Depp, Mickey Rourke, Nicolas Cage, and many others. Maybe it makes sense for you to pay attention to this system as well?

After all, what is the difference between a good actor and a bad or a mediocre actor? The difference is in that he/she fully transforms into a character he/she is playing. When he/she is acting, as an individual an actor/actress completely disappears and the audience sees a completely different person in his/her place—a person, who looks, stands, sits, walks, moves, eats, dresses, expresses emotions, and so on in a different way. In short, he/she does everything not like he/she "automatically" does it in everyday life. In a couple of words, this is the art of transformation[10].

Specifically the art of complete (ideally) transformation is required when acting out a scenario from any natural manipulation mode. Nothing else is needed. And, in order to do this it is not necessary to be born with some sort of gift—that is a fairy-tale. Potentially, every person can do this. All you need to do is simply to study and to practice.

Also, when working with a subject of manipulation it is recommended not to forget that it takes time, multiple repetitions, consistency and persistence on the part of a trainer to get even a dog to make some primitive actions. Therefore, the variant "play the role once and the subject of manipulation is yours forever" is something from your wild imagination. Yes, if you have only one chance to meet with a subject of manipulation and need to get something from him/her during this meeting—it is what it is, but anyway use of manipulation modes makes this task much, much easier. However, it is very naïve to dream that "in just one sitting" you can make a subject to manipulation "yours." In this sense a human is not any different from an animal.

*****

Now, a few words about what a manipulator will be able to observe if he/she plays the role from the suppression mode to people born on October 12th of leap years or October 13th of common years more or less correctly.

A person, toward whom someone is transmitting his personal suppression mode, relaxes and calms down, his mood changes from angry-dull-irritable to positive, he begins to smile and, of course, his attitude toward a manipulator is more than positive. In connection with this, a subject of manipulation perceives that what a manipulator suggests (wishes/asks for) more favorably. These are the reactions, which most likely you will be able to observe in reality, when you transmit toward people born on October 12th of leap years and October 13th of common years their natural suppression mode.

However, if you take on manipulation seriously, meaning—if you transmit toward him/her the suppression mode from all six factors and do it systematically for some time (for example, a month or two), then you will get that what is described in detail in Part 2 Chapter 4 of this book—a subject of manipulation might seriously fall in love with you, become attached to you, and then he/she really will fulfill any of your wishes.

Also, it is likely that you will be able to observe that people, who were born on October 12th of leap years or October 13th of common years, tend to behave as described in the scenario of their suppression mode. This is not surprising because manipulation modes, as it was mentioned above, are correctors of psychophysiological state of *Homo sapiens*, which a person uses unconsciously. We think that such observation will also be a good illustration for you of that we really do know how to get information from the unconscious sphere of *Homo sapiens* and that we do this without errors.

*****

No matter what you managed to get from a subject of manipulation by using his/her suppression mode, from the very start you should not even dream that under this influence a person will cardinally change or will become a different person. This is impossible in principle because *Homo sapiens* is a bio-robot with a built-in from birth subtype program as the sum of personal qualities, life algorithms, preferences, etc., beyond which he/she simply cannot go during his/her entire life.

Application of personal manipulation modes can easily make a subject of manipulation cardinally change his/her attitude toward you, motivate him/her to do something for you, to correct his/her behavior in the way that you want, but his/her nature will remain unchanged. It is possible to cardinally change a human, as a living mechanism, only by breaking him/her. However, we hope that a manipulator will use this tool with care and in a humane way, and will not forget that application of this tool— natural manipulation modes, which have such a serious, deep influence on human psychophysiology—makes you responsible for a person, whose soul is in your hands.

*****

In conclusion, we can add that additional information about people, who were born on October 12th of leap years and October 13th of common years, about their manipulation modes and about how to manipulate them is available from a recording of a live one hour long broadcast on Russian television (Sexual Revolution program on channel Televizionnyy Damskiy Klub [Ladies Club Television]), where a series of presentations about the Catalog of Human Population were made in 2005-2006, and one of them was about people, who belong to this subtype. This recording, as well as recordings about people, who were born on December 7th of common years, March 22nd of leap years and March 23rd of common years can be found on our website at http://www.humanpopulationacademy.org/olga-skorbatyuk-russian-television.

[1] If you cannot communicate with a subject of manipulation in person, then it can be done via the Internet: through social networks with messaging and chat systems, via Skype and other similar systems.

[2] Of course, you must take into account whether it was a leap year or a common year. For example, people born on October 13th of common years and people born on October 13th of leap years do not belong to the same subtype, and therefore have different programs and different manipulations modes. The situation is the same with people born on October 12th of common years and October 12th of leap years. However, people born on October 12th of leap years and October 13th of common years do belong to the same subtype.

[3] Verification (from Latin *verus* - true and *facio* - doing) means testing, empirical confirmation of theoretical positions of science by comparing them with observed objects, sensory data, experiment.

[4] This is not complete information, but it is quite enough, including for manipulation purposes. If you want to know more about a person you are interested in and how he/she can be controlled even more, you can purchase images, by which a particular manipulation mode is recorded. After studying images on your own, you will be able to get additional information and a lot of it. Information about where and how you can buy images of human programs and manipulation modes from the Catalog of Human Population is available in the Preface and at the end of each book of the Catalog of Human Souls series.

[5] In the case of manipulation modes of any one of two hundred and ninety three subtypes of human population, a manipulator "gets into" natural images of a subject(s) of manipulation. Information about how "getting into" these images affect a subject of manipulation is described in detail in Part 2 Chapter 4 of this book.

[6] Absolutely all descriptions of human "software" (of any subtype) from the Catalog of Human Population have the same structure: a general description of a person and information on six factors. However, there are some differences. Each analytical material that is provided to our clients, who purchase programs and manipulation modes of *Homo sapiens*, is not, so to speak, unisex like the scenario that we provided for testing of the suppression mode of people born on October 12th of leap years and October 13th of common years. Each one has "a gender" and is provided according to gender of a client or depending on a goal. It makes sense to know this for those, who plan to purchase information about themselves or other people from us. One can get a complete understanding of the form, in which a client receives a description of someone's individual program or manipulation mode from the suppression mode of people born on October 12th of leap years and October 13th of common years, which we provided in this book.

[7] All this information also relates to acting out the suppression mode of any other *Homo sapiens* subtype. This book does not include instructions on how to use the other two natural manipulation modes (balancing and stimulating). We provide instructions on how to do it only to those, who purchase information from the Catalog of Human Population, and only though consultations or distance learning at the Human Population Academy (http://www.humanpopulationacademy.org/pricing).

[8] Konstantin S. Stanislavsky is a Russian theater director, actor and teacher, reformer of theater. He created the famous acting system, which is very popular in Russia and around the world for already one hundred years.

[9] "I do not believe you!" – is a phrase that became legendary in the world of cinema, theater and in daily life, after Stanislavsky (see [8] above) began to use it as a director's technique.

[10] According to dictionaries, actor's transformation is the ability of an actor to change internally and externally. This phenomenon is a temporary transition of an actor "into reality" of a new person, someone else's "I"—into psyche and psychology of a different person and reproduction of this new "I" in the form of a specific image.

CHAPTER 2

SUPPRESSION MODE OF PEOPLE BORN ON OCTOBER 12ᵀᴴ OF LEAP YEARS AND OCTOBER 13ᵀᴴ OF COMMON YEARS
(Manipulation Scenario For Men And Women)

The following text is taken from the Catalog of Human Population. It is © 2005 Andrey Davydov, Olga Skorbatyuk. All rights reserved. Translation is © 2015 Kate Bazilevsky. All rights reserved.

This person (either a man or a woman) perceives himself/herself a titled person. If it is a woman, then she considers herself at least a duchess or a princess, but more likely an empress; and if it is a man, then his self-sentiment is that of a duke, a prince or an emperor. Regardless of who this person is in real life, no matter what social position he/she occupies—his/her self-sentiment is that of a ruler, a sovereign; moreover, a perfect ruler: kind, wise and, of course, outstanding, superior to all even if he/she is a cashier at a supermarket or live in a shelter for the homeless.

This individual might have no special knowledge or even a standard required education, no extraordinary talents or any skills at all. In any case, he/she behaves like a king or a queen always, everywhere and with everyone. This individual considers himself/herself a blue-blooded person, who is no match for all other people, and stubbornly believes that he/she has all thinkable qualities that exist in nature. Since, as it is known, the status of an emperor or an empress, as an expression of the essence of monarchical layer, claims the role of no more and no less than that of an intermediary between Heaven (God's will) and Earth (people).

That is ideally, but in real life similar mission is realized by very few monarchs, at least because usually they do not have some personal qualities that cardinally differentiate them from their lieges. Ideally, an emperor must be the etalon carrier and demonstrate to his lieges that sounding of personality, which would be consonant with "music of heaven." However, more often sovereigns of this level amount to despotic petty tyrants, capricious, with claims and try to implement self-legitimized unlimitedness based on the principle "I do as I want." Exactly the same behavior can be observed in this person.

This individual is similar to a capricious blue-blooded person, who, without being something special, only by the right of birth claims to rule over other people. He/she purports to do what he/she pleases and does not care about wishes of "some heaven." Execution of his/her personal will is much more important to him/her.

He/she considers himself/herself a person, who has qualities, which are the etalon for all other people, are exemplar, and most importantly—the reason for people to obey him/her unquestioningly. And, it does not even occur to him/her that these qualities might be far from real etalons. This is what he/she decided and it is quite enough.

In case someone doubts his/her dignities and superiority, if there is a need to prove his/her exclusivity to someone, then this person will stand up for himself/herself. He/she will, so to speak, dig the ground with his/her nose and do whatever it takes to prove that he/she really is above all in his/her dignities and qualities. Even if the proof will not seem too convincing to other people, this will not in any way affect his/her exorbitantly high self-rating and exorbitant ambitions. All doubts will be written off as stupidity of others and that they are simply unable to evaluate his/her dignities because they are nobodies and can only be nobodies.

Inside himself/herself this person clearly knows that he/she is superior to other people, better than they are, and therefore he/she is worthy to command, dominate, control, and rule over them. In this sense, it is a waste of time to try to change his opinion or to try to challenge his actions and decisions. This individual reasons very simply: "I consider myself wonderful no matter what, and this gives me every right to do what I want. And, all other people have the right to do only what I want."

Having this kind of sense of self, this person behaves accordingly—as a sovereign. It does not matter if he/she is heading to a board of directors meeting or to a store for some milk; it does not matter how he/she is dressed—in a suit that is worth tens of thousands of dollars and diamonds or sweatpants stretched out at the knees. It does not matter whether he is sitting in the back seat of a huge luxury limousine or is steering the wheel of some old car covered with corrosion. It does not matter how much money this person has in his/her bank account and whether he/she has access to gold reserves of a country or a just couple of crumpled dollars and some change in his wallet.

Even if he/she washes cars, sells gasoline at a gas station or wipes off other people's spits and scrubs off dried up gum at public restrooms—in any case, he/she will always find a way to show you who he/she is and who you are. For example, by his/her posture, voice, facial expressions, tone that he/she will use to talk to you. Or, he/she might pour a bucket of dirty water over your feet, as if by accident, and when you become outraged he/she will find a way to show you how insignificant you are compared to him/her.

In any situation, this person's posture is prideful, steps are measured, manners are regal, and his/her behavior is haughty, stately and patronizing. Just try not to get angry and make claims because if you do, you will see what it means to debate with a person, who thinks that he/she is a person of the highest rank! The main function of this person, as he/she sees it, is to rule and reign without limitations, meaning—as he/she pleases. This person regards other people as if he/she is on the throne and all others are at his/her feet.

This individual separates all matters into two categories: important—his/her own, and mere nothings—other people's. If in response to his/her demand to do something a person will try to resent and defend his rights or will try to convey to this him/her the simple fact that he also might have his own private affairs—he/she will simply glance in that person's direction with coldness and incomprehension, and nothing more. He/she just does not understand a situation, in which someone tries to contradict him/her or refuses to do that what he/she suggests.

This person thinks that other people are obligated to submit to all his/her demands and whims, including ridiculous ones. Especially since, as it seems to this person, he/she never makes absurd demands. And, this person does not bother to think about whether he/she makes correct decisions or not, does not care to burden himself/herself with how and in which form to demand something from a person. It is not characteristic of this person to take into consideration peculiarities, needs and desires of other people. He/she thinks that all of his/her decisions are wise to begin with, and therefore are correct.

He/she thinks that his/her personal affairs are of paramount importance and cannot wait, while any affairs of other people are simply trivial, not worth attention, as from his/her point of view, others are simply unable to do anything else. In general, he/she does not understand very well why he/she needs try to consider interests of other people, conform to them. His/her reasoning goes something like this: "Who are they compared to me?! Nothings, trash in the corner." This person is convinced that compared to him/her other people are simply nobodies, their names are nothings, and all of them exist only to execute his/her decrees, orders, commands, wishes, and for nothing more than this. And, they must execute unquestioningly and with a sense of admiration for him/her.

It is not enough for him/him that the surrounding people execute his/her decrees or requests (which, by the way, always have a shade of a demand, the highest order). It is desirable that after executing some actions, the surrounding people (whom this person considers his/her slaves, servants, vassals) would present him/her results on a golden plate and with a respectfully bowed head. It is not enough just to do something for this person—one also has to present it as a moment of personal happiness, something like: "Happy to serve!" That is, demonstrate to this person with all one's appearance that all of his/her instructions, wishes and whims were not only met, but were executed with joy and complete awareness of that it was an honor to execute them. While all actions in relation to others this individual sees as moments when he/she condescends to them and makes the greatest benefaction for them.

Another quality of considered individual is that this person makes the overall impression of a kind of a block, monolith, pillar, on which everything stands. And, he/she is not embarrassed to demonstrate his/her strength and might on all factors. In the intellectual factor, he/she is capable of generating far from ordinary thoughts and powerful ideas. In the physical factor, he/she is happy to demonstrate strong physique and physical strength. In the nutritional factor, he/she prefers energy-intensive food (meaning that he/she likes to eat a lot and a variety of delicious, hot, spicy foods). In the sexual factor, he/she is capable of, so to speak, shaking the bed so much that the downstairs neighbors' chandelier will swing. He/she thinks that a person, on whom everything around stands, as earth on the shoulders of Atlas, should not be any different and simply cannot behave in some other way.

Regardless of age and gender, this person considers himself/herself the great patron of everyone and everything, an enlightener, a teacher, capable of "bringing downtrodden and dark masses to light." This individual always appears before surrounding people as a person, who proclaims the ultimate truth. This is a consequence of his/her conviction that he/she knows the principles of true world order. Attempts to dissuade him/her are doomed to fail. In the best case, he/she will calmly, haughtily and arrogantly grant the opponent with a scornful look, as if saying: "Pal, you will never be able to reach my level!!" Considered individual inexorably, firmly holds his/her positions. Attempts of others to move him/her to the side or, god forbid, make him/her step aside, by their effectiveness will equal to attempts of moving a strong cliff—this is how much on the inside this person is convinced of his/her power, rightness and competency (on all positions).

This is precisely the reason that this individual always strives to be the leader of some community: from the head of the family to the head of an academic council, from the head of a land cooperative or a two people work team to the head of a major religious confession. In all spheres, he/she seeks to ensure that the main indication of his/her social position is his/her factual position "above" all other members of a community. This person not only strives to hold the position of the boss (no matter if it is his/her own liquor store or a large holding company), but also reinforces this desire by specific actions. For example, he/she makes great efforts in regard to his/her career and certainly will try to make way to the highest echelons of power. Most likely, he/she will do this in stages, step-by-step and move up the corporate ladder, obtaining more senior positions until he/she reaches the top.

Having extremely high ambitions, this person thinks that, for example, it is not right to remain a Ph.D. all his life since it is possible to become a professor. If education does not work out, then he/she will realize his "superstructure" over other people in some other way, but he/she certainly will try to do it. Also, throughout his/her life this individual strives to get into "high society," elite social circles, including aristocratic.

Moreover, possessing those ambitions and sense of self, which this person has by nature, if for any reason he/she fails to get a high social position (either because he/she will not make sufficient efforts to achieve this, or life circumstances will not allow), then he/she might fall catastrophically low. Under unfavorable circumstances, instead of high society, this individual might become a part of the homeless community and, in the best case, become a dethroned king/queen, who lost his/her throne, wealth and vassals, and in the worst case—a degraded, angry individual, who, to the bewilderment of others and for an unclear reason, poses as a blue-blooded person. Being a born triumphant, who expects only an unending chain of victories from his/her life, it will be very difficult for him/her to accept circumstances, which hinder his/her movement upward and realization of ambitious pursuits and aspirations to rule and reign.

Intellectual Factor

This person can be characterized as a classifier of all and everything—this person will divide the whole world, including society, by types and grades and surely will sort all information that comes in. Also, he/she sorts people by categories and does this only on the bases of his/her personal criteria. He/she considers categories through his/her personal prism and gives people various nicknames, sobriquets, using special jargon. For example, he/she might say something like this about someone: "This guy is clearly a neotrop" or "This woman is from the category of slow pokes." This person thinks up name-labels, nicknames, which get assigned to a particular category of people, himself/herself, for personal use, as if creating a special language like thieves' lingo or language of Tolkienists.

Also, this person tends to conduct comparative analysis of information.

He/she is a fan of logic and structure in the intellectual sense.

He/she is capable of regularly, for show deflating the level and volume of information that he/she has and pretending to be a complete idiot for some time.

He/she highly values a thought polished to perfection.

Getting a huge amount of information that literally flows to him/her from all sides, this person is not in a hurry to part with it—meaning, to share it with someone. He/she is convinced that it is always better to have information for personal use only. Thus, this person tends not only to accumulate information that he received from a variety of sources in himself/herself, but in a sense to rot it and with that arrange peculiar "informational constipations" by analogy with intestinal constipation.

Being stubborn and inflexible, this person has the following peculiarity: the lower the level of culture of this person, the bigger bullhead, ignoramus, and dullard he/she is. In this sense, solidity, as a natural quality of this person, can be very boring for others.

Physical Factor

In the physical factor, this person is very neat, tidy and "a fan of clean hands."

He/she has an insurmountable need to constantly clean, wash, and polish to a shine everything around him. For example, working at a bar, this person will make mirrors out of glasses. And, after wiping off crumbs from a kitchen table using some cloth, he/she will thoroughly wash it with soap, powder or some other cleanser before reusing it.

In his/her bathroom there is a razor (and not just one), as well as combs for parting hair and for hair on all other parts of his/her body.

This person necessarily has red things in his/her wardrobe; for example a shirt, a t-shirt, shorts, pants (skirt), shoes, a bag, underwear, etc.

He/she certainly uses various lubricating and wiping products for shoes and everything else that requires similar care. And, he/she makes no exception for himself/herself either—he/she uses a variety of creams. If there are no creams on hand, he/she might use regular petroleum jelly.

He/she loves to wear warm knitted garments, especially at home.

From precious and semi-precious stones he/she prefers malachite, garnet.

He/she might take a great interest in a wide variety of physical activities. For example, he/she might have a fancy for diving.

He/she tends to use medicines of mineral origin.

Nutritional Factor

In the nutritional factor, limitations do not exist for this person. He/she might not eat a lot of what can be found on his/her table, but there must be delicacies, splendid, various foods and a lot of them.

This person loves to eat small fish.

He/she is a fan of crabs.

He/she is not against having a seaweed salad.

This person is not against eating partridges, besides other meat delicacies.

At home, for himself/herself personally, he/she will keep coarsely ground rock salt.

He/she prefers to drink spring water, or at least water filtered through special filters.

From dairy products he/she prefers various yogurts.

He/she likes cottage cheese and dishes made of this product.

He/she regularly eats fresh greens, potatoes, cucumbers.

From spices he/she prefers ginger, as an additive to dishes.

He/she loves candies, especially chocolate ones.

Emotional Factor

This individual has the following peculiarity: if someone transmits emotions towards him/her quite strongly, and makes him/her enter any emotional state for a long period of time, then this emotion either gets returned to that same person or gets directed toward the first person he/she encounters.

For example, during communication with some person this man or woman got a charge of so-called "negative" emotions—someone upset or insulted him/her, swore at him/her, and so on. In this case, he/she certainly will immediately start to worry about this. This will manifest in that he/she will constantly try to remember how it all happened, who said what to him/her and what he/she responded. This person is simply incapable of just forgetting what happened, he/she is unable to pay no attention to it or not to worry about it.

Naturally, these worries will bring him/her down greatly, seriously affect his/her mood, well-being and all of his/her life activities in general. It is quite difficult to carry such a burden for a long time, but this person is unable to part with it quickly because he/she tends to dwell on any emotional state for a long time. Therefore, at the first opportunity he/she will surely try to throw some of his/her emotional weight on someone else. For example, he/she will want to talk to someone about what happened, complain or simply seek some compassion.

If the emotion that was directed at this individual was aggressive, then, in response, an explosive outbreak of aggression on part of this person is possible: either in relation to the one, who provoked this emotion in him/her, or in relation to some person he/she just happens to come across. Here, as the saying goes, "one who did not hide is the guilty." And, the emotion that arose in this person usually is several times stronger than the one that he/she received from the environment.

The same happens with this person in cases when he/she receives so-called "positive" emotions: for a rather long period of time he/she becomes remarkably inspired, experiences an emotional uplift, and he/she is ready, so to speak, "to jump for joy." And, of course, he/she always seeks to share his joy with someone.

If someone scares this person a little bit, then, after he/she stays in this emotion for some time, he/she will grow it to all-encompassing horror of enormous size. However, again he/she will surely share this nightmare with someone and discuss the situation, as this person always feels much better once he/she shares his/her emotional states with someone.

In short, in emotional exchanges with other people, this person demonstrates by his/her behavior that, figuratively speaking, you will ride a horse only as well as you harness it. And, without receiving emotions from the outside (from other people) this person is like a stone lying on the road: coldblooded, calm, indifferent.

Even though this individual can be characterized as a coldblooded person, he/she is capable of brief, but very strong emotional outbursts, which somewhat resemble fireworks (firecrackers). And, at such moments he/she might express himself/herself quite loudly, clamorously, and behave in a very unrestrained manner. At the same time, despite any of his/her emotional manifestations, he/she considers himself/herself a calm and balanced person, and this quite often amazes the surrounding people.

Sexual Factor

In the sexual factor, this person thinks that the period of courtship must be long and romantic.

If this is a woman, then she likes it when her admirer devotes poems to her or sings serenades under her window as a professional heartbreaker. She loves to get many signs of attentions and, of course, she loves gifts (especially, she likes to get necklaces). And, this woman does not like admirers, who are cheapskates when it comes to gifts. She herself might give gift to a man she is with because she likes not only to receive gifts, but to give them as well.

If this is a man, then he always pays many signs of attentions to his admirers and also always gives gifts. And, he gives gifts not because he is forced to do so, but because he does not respect men, who do not do this during courtship and does not want to be one of them. At the same time, he himself will never refuse to accept gifts from his mistress—it is always pleasant to him.

As for women, after the romantic period (which, as mentioned above, in the case of this woman is mandatory) she happily get marries. As for men, unlike many others, he is also ready to get married. (Of course, to a woman, who, in his opinion, is suitable to be his wife.) This happens because this person (a man or a woman) considers family a required, necessary element of his/her life.

Family is sacred to this person because all his/her life he/she wants to connect, unite, join his/her fate with someone. Therefore, it is imperative that he/she finds himself/herself a suitable partner to marry and create a family with.

After marriage, this person will always spend all of his/her vacation, holidays and weekends together with members of his/her family.

Regardless of gender, when living with his/her wife/husband, he/she will emphasize the word "we" in order to show the unbreakable unity of this pair. It is characteristic of this person to extol his/her choice of partner at every opportunity: "We are a perfect pair."

For this person (of any gender), the main reason for violation of faithfulness in marriage is the following natural peculiarity: he/she responds to any sexual calling from the environment that is directed at him/her very quickly and strongly. However, since he/she values his/her marriage union he/she might, as much as he/she can, try to avoid such situations, but it is difficult for him/her to go against this natural property.

This person perceives his/her son, if he/she has one, as an inheritor of a great dynasty, and his/her daughter—as a princess.

This person's relationship with his/her mother-in-law is interesting. He/she will continue to communicate with her regardless of what kind of a relationship they have (whether it is friendly or not), and will happily fight with his/her mother-in-law or just as happily communicate with her quietly and peacefully.

Regardless of gender, family life of this person gets built based on the principle of strict patriarchal rules—"Our dad is the most important." For example, in case of a man, he will expect/demand that his wife, children and other family members treat him like a king and a god even if by his social status "dad" in this household is a simple unskilled worker; and, he will expect from his wife to feel like a queen next to him.

This person gets very jealous. He/she gets jealous to the point that in a situation when someone is trying to take away his/her wife/husband, so to speak, right from under his/her nose, then he/she is capable of solving the problem cardinally—"If not for me, then for no one else."

Most likely, this individual will seek to know his/her family tree.

Environmental Factor

In the environmental factor, this person is convinced that he/she has remarkable talents in government affairs. Having a great interest in jurisdiction, he/she dreams about rewriting all existing laws because he/she considers himself/herself a brilliant lawmaker, capable of easily (like cookies in his/her kitchen) "molding" laws, by which the whole country will live.

This individual is a supporter of inviolable laws. For example, if he/she devotes himself/herself to religious activities, then he/she will advocate for strictness, inflexibility and immutability of moral, ethical and religious dogmas, norms, laws, etc.

If this person becomes an official, then, most likely he/she will be a classic bureaucrat: he/she will create a firm schedule of his/her activities and will pay a great deal of attention to existence and verification of all required documentation, according to the principle: "Without papers you're an insect, and with papers you are a human." This individual has special respect for stamps and mastics for them, as well as for identification cards, admission passes and other documents that confirm identity. He/she will also collect and carefully save all receipts and stubs.

At work this person has a tendency to complicate already existing connections and relationships within some system: interpersonal relationships, business, and so on. For example, if he/she is engaged in organization and management, then this individual will personally duplicate execution of his/her own orders. Supposedly, he/she will do this just in case.

In any activity, in any undertaking this individual can be characterized as a person, who is oriented towards participation in the process, and not reception of any kind of results. And, the process must be extended in time, endless. For example, if he/she is some sort of an official, he/she dreams of one thing only—to keep this position forever. He/she gives all of his/her strength to participation in this process, while there never were and never will be any specific steps taken to get results from his/her activities. This reminds of the behavior of a character from a famous book titled The Good Soldier Švejk (by Jaroslav Hašek)—courageous soldier Švejk, to whom it was not important where to go and where he will eventually arrive because more important is to always be en route.

In all spheres of his/her life and activities this person will implement a single principle, which he/she is guided by on all factors: "Divide et impera!" (Lat. "Divide and rule!"). In addition to aspiration to rule, he/she still always seeks to divide everything into zones and implement control over each one. When it comes to people, he/she will first try to separate them all, divide them up, so that he/she could rule over them and keep the situation under personal control.

Also, this person has the ability of a perfect communicator, who connects people with each other. In this case, he/she gets an opportunity to lead communication streams that pass through him/her. This attracts him/her very much, as he/she considers himself/herself the main connecting link in any relationships between people. Also, he/she considers it important to always know secret and open information.

As for the sphere of his/her professional activities, here too this person will divide up his/her territory into segments, which he/she will control at his/her own discretion. He/she is a big fan of all sorts of inspection trips, business trips with the goal of checking territories, which he/she controls. This person really likes the role of an inspector-general. These trips give him/her a reason to feel his/her importance, and also such function gives him/her the possibility and the right to regularly intervene in affairs and private lives of other people, to control their actions. Therefore, once he/she gets a territory under its control, he/she will accurately, firmly perform his/her duties.

This individual cherishes his/her territories, being guided by the following principle: "I will not give away even an inch of my native land!" Even if it is not a country with huge territories, but rather a small, for example, backyard—this person (regardless of gender) might organize a great battle over one-thousandth of his/her territory, on which, for example, his/her enemy-neighbor planted a flower or set a piece of wood. And, if it so happens that this, conditionally speaking, bush or a flower grows on a territory that does not belong to anyone at all, then this will become the reason for this person to consider this tiny piece of land as his/her own, his/her property. He/she will capture it quickly, promptly, and loudly, in the event that neighbors decide to defend their rights for this patch of land.

If he/she lives in, for example, a small room, then this person will also divide the space into sections. He/she will use sections of this unit in various ways, depending on what functionality he/she will determine for particular space. For example: "I sleep here", "I work here", "and, in this corner, I receive guests." As a consequence of this, his/her entire room might be divided into sectors by the use of various items: screens, shelves, curtains, cabinets, partitions, and so on. However, for a person with imperial ambitions, living in a small room, of course, is not very desirable.

As far as this individual's preferences in regard to housing—he/she will be quite content to reside in a house, even if it does not belong to him/her, but in which titled people live. For example, if he/she becomes an excellent professional in the field of arts, like Mr. Piotrovsky, then he/she can very well live in the Hermitage Museum (in Saint Petersburg), even without it being his/her personal property.

There is a peculiarity. On the one hand, this person is able to make his/her home (if funds allow) a royal palace and sometimes go outside the limits of good taste due to his/her desire for flashy luxury. And, on the other hand, if he/she does not have a place with rich interior due to lack of sufficient financial resources, then he/she can be satisfied by modest simplicity of the interior and by that provide himself/herself another luxury—the luxury of simplicity. In this case, he/she will organize his/her home based on the following principle: "simple-rough-functional."

By the way, being a big fan of all kinds of extremes, this individual always balances on the verge of rising and falling. For example, at times this person does everything to look super-luxurious and lead a super-luxurious lifestyle (all the way to the extent that life beyond his/her available financial means literally destroys him/her), and then starts to lean towards minimalism and simplicity in everything. Sometimes he/she makes everything around him/her so clean and ordered that it all sparkles and shines, and at other times he/she produces a lot of trash around him/her and becomes literally overgrown with mold and covered with dust.

This person has a stable desire to live well, peacefully, calmly. He/she will seek to have his/her own house, but taking into account imperial ambitions of this individual—preferably in the form of his/her own huge cottage or a villa with awnings, cornice, veranda. (This person thinks that if his/her house is not a royal palace, then it must at least resemble one.)

As for the house itself, this person thinks that it must necessarily have stone foundation, or even better—to be completely made of stone (at worse—of bricks). The interior might contain encaustic tiles, and everything possible will be lined with stone tiles. Also, he/she thinks that it would be good if on the territory that belongs to him/her would be a path laid out of cobblestones. A pond or a lake in the yard is also desirable, so that during the appropriate season of the year it would be possible to swim and sunbathe at his/her private beach.

This individual pays a great deal of attention to protection of his/her private property, whether it is a small rented apartment or a huge private territory with a palace and adjacent structures. In the first case, he/she will insist on at least the most simple security system, while in the second—on installation of latest and super-powerful devices for monitoring and protecting the territory. Especially since, if funds are available, he/she will certainly seek to have a personal treasury. This can be a small-sized box, into which he/she will put the most precious items, or a large fire-proof safe.

This person thinks that books are good when there are a lot of them and they all have expensive, posh bindings. And, the more books there are in his/her house—the better.

Graphics, black and white photography attract him/her.

He/she is a fan of mosaic panels, plaster statuettes, products made out of stone.

He/she loves black smooth lacquered surfaces in the interior. This can be furniture, Chinese lacquered screens, Japanese lacquered boxes, Russian Palekh boxes and other similar items.

This person pays attention to small items, which he/she can sedulously collect, and devote quite a lot of his/her free time to it: netsuke, stamps, coins, tiny toy soldiers, etc.

In his/her youth, seeking to be a monocratic master everywhere, this person will try to live on his/her own, separately from his/her parents. For this purpose, he/she might rent his/her own place. Later on, if for some reason he/she will be left all alone (for example, if his/her wife/husband left him or died, and children grew up and started their own families), he/she will divide up his/her property into small rooms and will happily rent them out. Since in this case he/she gets the opportunity to manage his/her tenants, push them around, control their lives, etc. That is exactly why this person can become a wonderful owner of inns, apartment buildings, hotels or motels.

This person might become interested in stones. He/she can either professionally engage with mineralogy, or become an avid collector of stones. His/her collection will necessarily include precious stones. Or, he/she can become an excellent grinder of precious stones, a gem cutter.

Also, he/she might engage in funeral business, become a manager of, for example, a funeral facility, etc. This kind of occupation can attract this person because of his/her natural passion for packaging all and everything: from a sandwich (first, wrapped in foil, then put into a bag, and then into a container) to burial of people. In relation to himself/herself, depending on his/her social and financial situation, this individual will dream either of his/her own mausoleum, where his/her body will rest after death, or at least of a small family burial vault at a cemetery.

He/she can become quite a good sculptor.

He/she can become a woodcarver, a good restorer of furniture (and this will allow him/her to skillfully make fakes).

This person can get seriously passionate about music. Out of all musical genres, ceremonial sounding of hymns and chorales attracts him/her most of all. However, he/she might also find rhythmic modern music attractive. If since childhood this person was engaged in getting a musical education, then he/she will be able to become a good singer with repertoire ranging from chanson to pop. In this case, sooner or later he/she will compose music for himself. Being a nonprofessional, he/she might perform romances and songs during family holidays. He/she is capable of becoming a very good songwriter. Once he/she begins to compose music, he/she will then move on to composing texts.

During the period of thinking about his/her financial well-being, this person might direct his/her attention to the oil business, as one of the most profitable, and if there is a real opportunity to participate in it—he/she will definitely use this opportunity.

Seeking communication where the spirit of aristocratism dominates, he/she might find the path of a diplomatic worker attractive. And, in this field, he/she can achieve impressive successes. By the way, he/she values diplomacy in others in cases when these people are addressing him/her.

This person can become a great specialist in the field of architecture, design and art history. He/she likes to explore achievements of prominent people in this field. He/she finds particularly attractive pompous constructions of temples, castles of most different time periods. He/she could become a great designer. As an architect, this person is capable of satisfying the most refined tastes of aristocracy. Despite his/her fancy for a pompous style, he/she might very inventively synthesize pomposity and functionality in a style most suitable for modernity. He/she thinks that in planning and design everything must be beautiful, and exquisite, and very functional at the same time—that is, convenient.

As for rest time, this individual likes to vacation by the lakes. This territory can be similar to Switzerland, but necessarily have rivers, oxbow lakes and lakes. At the same time, he/she is not against vacationing in Thailand.

In general, as far as lifestyle, this person is firmly oriented on the West and the American way of life.

There is a peculiarity. It might take him/her a long time to begin taking active steps in any direction. At the same time he/she might allow himself to relax while smoking "a joint."

This person always clearly plans out all of his/her actions, and then quietly, calmly, but inexorably brings these plans to life. Once he/she implements yet another plan, he/she will surely report to himself: what was done, what was not done, and what were the results. Any plans, of course, tend to come to an end, but not for this individual—he/she always has many plans.

Considered individual is a secret or an open supporter of monarchy as a system, the monarchic power with all its attributes. He/she can become a supporter of the regal or royal house of the country, in which he/she lives. He/she might be interested in heraldry as a field of study, as well as a professional occupation. However, carried away by the pomposity of architectural styles, strictness of the Greek temples, inspection of how a festive table was served at a diplomatic reception, or by social lives of queens, princesses, dukes and counts—in all this, he/she finds attractive primarily mechanisms of power and what fruits they bear to those, who firmly hold this power in their hands.

As for relationships with other, this person considers it a norm to declare that he/she is all for strong unbreakable friendship. However, he/she can easily resort to vileness, and many years of friendship and long-term partnership will not stop him/her.

Moreover, knowing someone well enough this person loves to press on this person's "painful spots," meaning vulnerable points, and to feel a pleasant sense of power from that the poor person is literally warped and experiences many negative feelings at this moment. However, at the same time this person is very cautious. He/she will not allow that the person whom he/she maltreated begins to take revenge on him/her and his/her immediate family.

Also, this individual will always take care of security through patronage of influential people from different social strata.

One of peculiarities of this person (regardless of gender) is well reflected in the following saying: "I'm not vindictive; I simply have a good memory." This person also has very good memory; and especially of offenders and situations, in which he/she got insulted and humiliated. A lot of such situations occur throughout his/her life and this person collects them. He/she does this in order to remember some incident and put it in his own system of negative values. Regularly obtained unpleasant situations get compared to an already existing system, and if the situation is similar, then he/she has a response already. And this, he/she thinks, is very advantageous since it is not necessary to think up an answer.

By the way, this person does not care what to respond to an insult, he/she is only concerned about the degree of harshness in the response. If there was not enough harshness, then this individual becomes very upset. This person always suffers if it seems to him/her that his/her revenge was not enough because another convenient opportunity for revenge might not present itself. At the same time, if his/her opponent (the offender) is grand and powerful, or is similar to some person from the past, when he/she was unable to take revenge, then this person tries to avoid such situations. Since experiencing such humiliation (meaning, not being able to take revenge) is a very big trauma for this individual.

Also, this person enjoys games of chance very much. He/she likes to play checkers, chess, and cards.

The rest of information about October 12 leap years—October 13th common years subtype structure, relating to properties, algorithms and methods of self-regulation (control/management from the outside) is in other manipulation modes or archetypal components of the individual program.

Despite that clients, who purchase information about any of manipulation modes from our laboratory, usually receive it according to their gender (meaning: men get a male scenario, and women—a female scenario)—we had to make an exception to this rule in this demo scenario in order to make it practically usable for both genders.

CHAPTER 3

A CHEAPSKATE PAYS TWICE

Let's assume that you applied the suppression mode of people born on October 12th of leap years or October 13th of common years on practice. If you did not improvise and acted according to recommendations provided in Part 3 Chapter 1, then you got some results, despite that you are a beginner in working with natural "software" of *Homo sapiens* and particularly with manipulation modes.

For example, you saw a reaction of someone, who was born on these dates to his/her suppression mode and got something from this person. No matter what exactly: "a sudden outbreak" of sympathy in a subject of manipulation toward you, his/her interest in something you said/suggested/asked for or something material. And, the more qualitatively and the greater number of times you acted out the suppression mode to a person born on October 12th of leap years or October 13th of common years—the more you achieved.

Either way, we would like to draw your attention to a very important point in relation to application of manipulation modes of *Homo sapiens*. Probably, you do not know this yet. A person should not think that after playing the role from the natural suppression mode of a subject of manipulation to him/her (no matter how many times)—he/she "got him/her for good."

This is possible to do only in one case—when a manipulator has information about all three manipulation modes of a subject of manipulation (suppressing, balancing and stimulating), knows this person's individual program and images, by which natural "software" of a subject of manipulation is recorded in his/her psyche. Other ways to turn a human into a one hundred percent controllable machine simply do not exist in nature.

Management/control of *Homo sapiens* using the tool called "natural manipulation modes," figuratively speaking, is a car with four wheels. After all, the structure of human psyche consists of four parts: an individual program and three manipulation modes. And, if a manipulator wants "to ride" only using one wheel of this "manipulation car," then he/she must clearly understand that results will not be of that extent and degree, of which they could be because he/she simply does not have all the tools.

Mother Nature created not one, but three control modes of *Homo sapiens*. And, in order to control a human, besides the suppression mode it is also necessary to have a tool to gain his/her trust, and a tool to balance him/her, and a tool to stimulate (motivate) him/her to some actions. It is impossible to solve all this using only the suppression mode.

Yes, by having a scenario of only one manipulation mode of a person (especially the suppression mode), a manipulator can get a lot from a subject of manipulation by applying this mode. For example, a manipulator can get a subject of manipulation to perceive him/her as a very valuable and desirable person, who's wishes must be fulfilled. Of course, this is not bad already, but when it comes to application of manipulation modes in order to make a subject of manipulation one hundred percent controllable— application of just one manipulation mode is not enough.

In order to control a person with a guaranteed result, in addition to information about three manipulation modes of a subject of manipulation, a manipulator must know the individual (subtype) program of this person. What for? First of all, in order to be able to understand what to expect from a subject of manipulation and what not to expect, what to demand from him/her and what does not make sense to demand from him/her. This way a manipulator will not expect that one day, figuratively speaking, a horse will fly like a bird and a tiger will swim like a fish.

Secondly, knowledge of the individual program of a subject of manipulation also allows a manipulator to know exactly what reactions this particular person might have to particular manipulative actions. It happens that without being aware of individual natural particularities of a subject of manipulation, a manipulator assesses his/her reactions incorrectly and difficulties with modeling his/her behavior arise due to this. Or, when observing reactions of a subject of manipulation, a manipulator thinks that manipulation failed, but in fact a person reacted, and vice versa.

Thirdly, the natural individual program of a subject of manipulation also can be acted out for him/her as a scenario with manipulation purposes. Knowledge of the individual (subtype) program of a person used as a manipulation scenario allows a manipulator not only to attract attention of a subject of manipulation and get on his/her right side, but also to force him/her to consider a manipulator "one of his own", "genuinely closest." After all, in this case, a manipulator plays for a subject of manipulation his/her own self, talks to him in the language of his/her natural program, his/her unconscious. No one is able to resist such influence.

There are other ways to use knowledge of the individual program of a subject of manipulation. We touched upon this in the second book of the Catalog of Human Souls series titled Hack Anyone's Soul. 100 Demos Of Human Programs From The Catalog Of Human Population in practical examples of how the Catalog of Human Population differs from a horoscope. However, that is a different topic.

Probably it is not necessary to tell about why a manipulator needs to know natural images of the individual program and manipulation modes of a subject of manipulation because we already provided, from our point of view, a full answer to this question in Part 2 Chapter 4 of this book, in which we illustrated why and on what basis one person suddenly begins to obey another.

No matter if someone likes this or not, manipulation of a human is a very delicate mechanism. Psyche of *Homo sapiens* is not "a mystery;" it can be compared to a super-complicated lock, which is useless to try to open with pins or keys from other locks, regardless of the professional level of "a hacker." The key to each subject of manipulation is unique (his/her natural individual manipulation modes) and either a manipulator has the key to the "lock," which he/she decided to open, or he does not.

However, you will have to pay for "keys" (meaning—for information that turns a subject of manipulation into a machine that fully obeys you), as they are not being provided for free. And, each person will have to decide for himself/herself what level of influence he/she wants to have on someone and benefits he/she wants to get. After all, unlike a regular car, "a manipulation car" will ride on just "one wheel"; and, we hope that you will be able to make sure of this absolutely for free. However, the level of influence and the range of actions, which can be done to a subject of manipulation, and therefore results, which a manipulator will be able to achieve will vary significantly in comparison to "riding on all four wheels."

Moreover, over twenty years of practical application of the Catalog of Human Population clearly showed that by investing his/her personal financial means in information about a subject of manipulation, a manipulator not only always gets a return on his/her investment, but also gets much, much more than he/she invested.

However, this is not even a question of correctly choosing a subject for this kind of investment (since today there are over twenty million people in world, to each of whom the same manipulation mode from the Catalog of Human Population can be applied), but it is a question of goals that a manipulator sets. Depending on what a manipulator wants from a subject of manipulation, he/she can choose a rich, wealthy person and a person, who is, "as naked as a picked bone," from whom there is simply nothing to take.

Despite that managing/controlling someone using manipulation modes is a fun and a very profitable (from any point of view) process, it is not recommended to forget that just like you are manipulating someone today—you will be manipulated tomorrow. Or, you are already being manipulated, but you are not aware of this since it is impossible for you to figure out that someone is controlling you by using your manipulation modes. And, in this civilization, unfortunately, people are far from ideals of the so-called "universal love;" people manage to be kind and decent in relation to one another only in words, and even that they do not do very convincingly.

Investing your personal finances in order to gain control over someone else's soul and getting profits from this, of course, is wonderful. However, perhaps at the same time you should think about your favorite self and ensure your personal safety by investing in yourself? After all, no one is forbidden to receive information from the Catalog of Human Population about their own personal manipulation modes.

What will you gain? Knowledge of a person's own natural manipulation modes not only helps him/her finally become aware of and understand inner hidden unconscious motives, which make him/her submit to the will of others, fall in love with them, "firmly" get attached to them, do what others want and so on, but at some point it makes him/her unattainable for any manipulations.

Yes, for some time knowledge of your own natural manipulation modes will not free you from reflex reactions to transmissions of these modes from the outside. And, there is nothing you can do about this because manipulation modes are a built-in natural mechanism, which cannot be "uninstalled" or turned off. However, from the very beginning a person, who knows his/her manipulation modes (and, what is no less important—knows natural images, by which these modes are recorded in the unconscious) gets the opportunity to choose between obeying demands of a manipulator and "getting off the hook after eating the bait." And, this is a significant benefit.

When a person knows his/her individual natural program and manipulation modes, sooner or later he/she becomes absolutely autonomous and totally inaccessible for any manipulations from the outside. However, in this book it does not make sense to discuss how to achieve this. It makes sense to do this only with those people, who already have information about their natural program and manipulation modes.

It is useless to talk about this with all other people because now, automatically, they become a just a resource. After all, any person, who wants to manipulate them and invests his/her money in this will easily clean them out, take everything from them, and use them in all other senses of the word as well. Here, the famous saying "a cheapskate pays twice" fits well. However, we are not criticizing anyone in any way. Every person has the right to save money on himself/herself, even when he/she knows that one not so fine day he/she will have to pay for this and pay a lot.

The discovery of the Catalog of Human Population made by Andrey Davydov is so valuable because it gives a person the right to decide whether to continue to live like before or to make his/her life bright, lush, interesting, full, diverse, and resultative; to continue being who you are now or to become rich, healthy and happy "in one bottle" and to be free. Every person has the right to be whoever he wants to be and to live as he likes. Every person has the right to make a mistake, every person has the right to use other people's mistakes, but every person got the right to correct his/her mistakes.

BIBLIOGRAPHY

Vasilyev, V. P. (1866). *Analiz kitayskikh iyeroglifov (Sostavlen dlya rukovodstva studentov professorom S.-Peterburgskogo universiteta Vasilyevym)* [Analysis Of Chinese Hieroglyphs (Prepared By Professor Vasilyev Of University Of St. Petersburg To Guide Students)]. St. Petersburg.

Georgiyevskiy, S. M. (1892). *Mificheskiye vozzreniya i mify kitaytsev (s tablitsami kitayskikh iyeroglifov)* [Mythical Views And Myths Of The Chinese (With Tables Of Chinese Hieroglyphs)]. St. Petersburg: Tipografiya I. N. Skorokhodova.

Hall, M. P. (1928). *The Secret Teachings Of All Ages: An Encyclopedic Outline Of Masonic, Hermetic, Qabbalistic and Rosicrucian Symbolical Philosophy.* San Francisco: H.S. Crocker Company, Inc. Scanned November 2001, by Hare, J. Retrieved September 10, 2014, from http://www.framsteget.net/gratis/TheSecretTeachingsOfAllAges.pdf.

Yanshina, E. M. (Trans.). (1977). *Katalog Gor I Morej (Shan Hai Tszin)* [Catalog of Mountains and Seas (Shan Hai Jing)]. Moscow: Nauka.

Losev, A. F., Meletinskii, E. M., Riftin, B. L., Toporov, V. N., Ivanov, V. V., Averintsev, S. S., ... Afanasyeva, V. K. (1980). S. A. Tokarev (Ed.). *Mify narodov mira* [Myths of the World] (Vols. 1-2.). Moscow: Sovetskaya Entsiklopediya.

Sovetskiy Entsiklopedicheskiy Slovar' (SES) [Soviet Encyclopedic Dictionary]. (2nd ed.). (1982). Moscow: Sovetskaya Entsiklopediya.

Oshanin, I. M. (Ed.). (1983). *Bol'shoy kitaysko-russkiy slovar' (BKRS)* [Large Chinese-Russian Dictionary (BKRS)] (Vols. 1-4.). Moscow: Nauka.

Frazer, J. G. (1984). M. K. Ryklin (Trans.). *The Golden Bough: A Study In Magic And Religion.* Moscow: Politizdat. (Original work published 1890 under the title *The Golden Bough: A Study in Comparative Religion.*)

Pavlenko, N. A. (1987). *Istoriya pis'ma* [History of Writing]. Minsk: Vysheyshaya Shkola.

Starostin, S. A. (1989). *Rekonstruktsiya drevnekitayskoy fonologicheskoy sistemy* [Reconstruction Of The Ancient Chinese Phonological System.]. Moscow: Nauka.

Jung, C. G. (1991). A. M. Rutkevich (Ed.). *Arkhetip i simvol* [Archetype And Symbol]. Moscow: Renessans.

Shchutsky, J. K. (1993). A. I. Kobzev (Ed.). *Kitayskaya klassicheskaya "Kniga peremen"* [Chinese Classical Book of Changes]. (2nd ed.). Moscow: Vostochnaya Literatura.

Gariaev, P. P. (1994). *Volnovoy genom* [Wave Genome]. Moscow: Obshchestvennaya Polza. ISBN 9785856170053 ISBN 9785856171005 [Available at libraries http://www.worldcat.org/title/volnovoi-genom/.]

Lukyanov, A. E. (1994). *Nachalo drevnekitayskoy filosofii: "I tszin", "Dao de tszin", "Lun' yuy"* [The Beginning Of The Ancient Chinese Philosophy: I Ching, Tao Te Ching, Lun Yu]. Moscow: Radiks. ISBN 9785864630266. [Available at multiple libraries http://www.worldcat.org/title/nachalo-drevnekitaiskoi-filosofii-i-tszin-dao-de-tszin-lun-iui/.]

Davydov, A., & corr. of ITAR-TASS Fedoruk, V. (1998). Corr. of RAO L. Verbitskaya & Assoc. Prof. B. Sokolova (Eds.), *Pervyy Rossiyskiy Filosofskiy Kongress: Chelovek – Filosofiya – Gumanizm* [First Russian Philosophical Congress. Human Being – Philosophy – Humanism]: *Vol. 7 Philosophy and Human Problem: Is Shan Hai Jing The Original Catalog Of Psychophysiological Human Structure?* St. Petersburg: Saint Petersburg State University Publishing House, 7, 355-357. ISBN 9785288018947. Presentation at the First Russian Philosophical Congress: Human Being – Philosophy – Humanism (in Russian), St. Petersburg (1997). [Available at: University of Michigan http://mirlyn.lib.umich.edu/Record/003947324 B4231.R6751997 (subscription required), St. Petersburg's Central City Public Library Named After V. V. Mayakovsky http://www.pl.spb.ru/structure/zali/ ББК87Ч-391 (subscription required), and multiple other libraries http://www.worldcat.org/title/chelovek-filosofiia-gumanizm-pervyi-rossiiskii-filosofskii-kongress/]

Otyugov, A. A. (1998). Corr. of RAO L. Verbitskaya & Assoc. Prof. B. Sokolova (Eds.), *Pervyy Rossiyskiy Filosofskiy Kongress: Chelovek – Filosofiya – Gumanizm* [First Russian Philosophical Congress. Human Being – Philosophy – Humanism]: *Vol. 7 Philosophy and Human Problem: Psychological Nature Of Mythological Consciousness.* St. Petersburg: SPSU Publishing House. ISBN 9785288018947. Presentation at the First Russian Philosophical Congress: Human Being – Philosophy – Humanism (in Russian), St. Petersburg. Retrieved from http://mirlyn.lib.umich.edu/Record/003947324 B4231.R6751997 (subscription required). [Also available at other libraries http://www.worldcat.org/title/chelovek-filosofiia-gumanizm-pervyi-rossiiskii-filosofskii-kongress/.]

Torchinov, E. A. (1998). *Religii mira. Opyt zapredel'nogo (transpersonal'nyye sostoyaniya i psikhotekhnika).* [Religions of the World. Experience of the Transcendence (Transpersonal States and Psychotechnique)]. St. Petersburg: Tsentr "Peterburgskoye Vostokovedeniye". ISBN 9785858030782 [Available at libraries http://www.worldcat.org/title/religii-mira-opyt-zapredelnogo-transpersonalnye-sostojanija-i-psihotehnika/.]

Zarochentsev, K. D., & Khudyakov, A.I. (1998). Corr. of RAO L. Verbitskaya & Assoc. Prof. B. Sokolova (Eds.), *Pervyy Rossiyskiy Filosofskiy Kongress: Chelovek – Filosofiya – Gumanizm* [First Russian Philosophical Congress. Human Being – Philosophy – Humanism]: *Vol. 7 Philosophy and Human Problem: The Crisis Of Modern Psychodiagnostics*. St. Petersburg: SPSU Publishing House. ISBN 9785288018947. Presentation at the First Russian Philosophical Congress: Human Being – Philosophy – Humanism (in Russian), St. Petersburg. Retrieved from http://mirlyn.lib.umich.edu/Record/003947324 B4231.R6751997 (subscription required). [Also available at other libraries http://www.worldcat.org/title/chelovek-filosofiia-gumanizm-pervyi-rossiiskii-filosofskii-kongress/.]

Davydov, A., & Fedoruk, V. (1999). *Shan Khay Tszin: Mify Ili Struktura Psikhiki?* [Shan Hai Jing: Myths Or Structure Of Psyche?]. Moscow: *Power Of Spirit*, 32-35.

Davydov, A. (2002). *Katalog Chelovecheskoy Populyatsii* [*Catalog of Human Population*]. Presentation at the International Conference on Prospects of Preservation and Development of Unified Civilization of the Planet: Culture, Ecology, Cosmos (in Russian), Moscow (2002). [Mention in *Parlamentskaya Gazeta*: "...The most luminous were reports by ... A. Davydov about the program that he developed, which opens up the best, but often hidden qualities of a human..." (Umorov, I. (2002). *Chelovechestvu Otpushcheno Tol'ko Tri Goda* [Humanity Has Only Three Years]. Moscow: *Parlamentskaya Gazeta, Sphere of Reason*, 129 (1008), para. 4. Retrieved 13 May 2015 from http://old.pnp.ru/archive/10082921.html.)]

Ezhov, V. V. (2003). *Mify Drevnego Kitaya* [Myths of Ancient China]. (Ill. *Myths of Nations of the World*) Moscow: Astrel.

Wilhelm, R., & Wilhelm H. (2003). V.B. Kurnosova (Trans.). *Ponimaniye «I tszin». Antologiya.* [Understanding The I Ching. Anthology.]. (2nd ed.). *Tradition, Religion, Culture.* Moscow: Aleteya.

Terentev-Katansky, A. (2004). *Illyustratsii k kitayskomu bestiariyu: Mifologicheskiye zhivotnyye drevnego Kitaya* [Illustrations to Chinese Bestiary: Mythological Animals of Ancient China]. St. Petersburg: Forma T.

Nikitina, T. N., & Zaytsev, V.P. (Eds.). (2009). *Slovar' drevnekitayskikh iyeroglifov = 古代漢語字典: s prilozheniyem slovarya naiboleye chastotnykh omografov, vstrechayushchikhsya v drevnekitayskom tekste, sost. Ye. G. Ivanovoy* [The Dictionary Of Ancient Chinese Hieroglyphs = 古代漢語字典: With The Appended Dictionary Of Most Frequent Homographs Found In Ancient Chinese Text, Compiled By E. G. Ivanova]. St. Petersburg: Karo. ISBN 9785992504293

Davydov, A., & Skorbatyuk, O. (2014). K. Bazilevsky (Trans.). *AHNENERBE—Your Killer Is Under Your Skin* (Composed 2014. Original work published 2014 in Russian, ISBN 9781311356741.). San Diego, CA: HPA Press. ISBN 9781311266682

Davydov, A., & Skorbatyuk, O. (2014). K. Bazilevsky (Trans.). *IDEOLOGY OF RELIGIONS. Scientific Proof Of Existence Of "God": The Catalog Of Human Population.* (Original work published 2014 in Russian, ISBN 9781311946690.). San Diego, CA: HPA Press. ISBN 9781311413932 ISBN 9780988648593

OUR OTHER BOOKS RELATED TO OUR SCIENTIFIC RESEARCH

Monographic Series

Archetypal Pattern. Fundamentals of Non-Traditional Psychoanalysis.

Davydov, A., & Skorbatyuk, O. (2014). K. Bazilevsky (Ed.). Anonymous (Trans.). *Archetypal Pattern. Fundamentals of Non-Traditional Psychoanalysis*: *Vol. 1. From Carl Gustav Jung's Archetypes of the Collective Unconscious to Individual Archetypal Patterns*. (Composed 2005. Original work published 2013 in Russian, ISBN 9781301447688.). San Diego, CA: HPA Press. ISBN 9781311820082

Davydov, A., & Skorbatyuk, O. (2014). K. Bazilevsky (Trans.). *Archetypal Pattern. Fundamentals of Non-Traditional Psychoanalysis*: *Vol. 2. Can Archetypal Images Contain Chimeras?* (Composed 2005. Original work published 2013 in Russian, ISBN 978130184859.). San Diego, CA: HPA Press. ISBN 9781310658570

Davydov, A., & Skorbatyuk, O. (2014). Arkhetipicheskiy Pattern. Osnovy Netraditsionnogo Psikhoanaliza [Archetypal Pattern. Fundamentals of Non-Traditional Psychoanalysis]: *Vol. 3. Archetype Semantics: How This Corresponds to the Concept of an 'Image'. How Archetypal Are Images?* (Composed 2005.). Marina Del Rey, CA: Catalog Of Human Souls GP. ISBN 9781301337309

Davydov, A., & Skorbatyuk, O. (2014). K. Bazilevsky (Trans.). *Archetypal Pattern. Fundamentals of Non-Traditional Psychoanalysis*: *Vol. 4. Society As A Community Of Manipulators And Their Subjects*. (Composed 2005. Original work published 2013 in Russian, ISBN 9781301399901.). San Diego, CA: HPA Press. ISBN 9781311809353

Catalog of Human Population - Non-Fiction Series

Individual (Subtype) Human Programs

Davydov, A., & Skorbatyuk, O. (2013). *Katalog Chelovecheskikh Dush: Programmnoye Obespecheniye Dushi Muzhchin/Zhenshchin, Rodivshikhsya <Data>* [Catalog of Human Souls: Software of Soul of Men/Women Born On <Date>] (Vols. 1-218. In Russian. Composed 2005-

2013.). Marina Del Rey, CA: Catalog Of Human Souls GP. [Available at http://www.humanpopulationacademy.org/pricing/ in all languages].

Human Manipulation Modes

Davydov, A., & Skorbatyuk, O. (2013-2014). *Katalog Chelovecheskikh Dush: Kak Podchinit' Muzhchin/Zhenshchin, Rozhdonnykh <Data>. Zhenskiy/Muzhskoy Manipulyativnyy Ctsenariy.* [Catalog of Human Souls: How To Subdue Men/Women Born On <Date>. Female/Male Manipulation Scenario.] (Vols. 1-39. In Russian. Composed 2005-2013.). Marina Del Rey, CA: Catalog Of Human Souls GP. [Available at http://www.humanpopulationacademy.org/pricing/ in all languages].

Ideologies

Davydov, A. (2014). K. Bazilevsky (Trans.). *Terrorism: A Concept For The ATC (The Commonwealth Of Independent States Anti-Terrorism Center).* (Composed 2001. Original work published 2014 in Russian, ISBN 9781311277848.). San Diego, CA: HPA Press. ISBN 9781310032189

Davydov, A. (2014). K. Bazilevsky (Trans.). *Ideology Of Monarchy. For Office Of The Head Of The Russian Imperial House, Her Imperial Highness Grand Duchess Maria Vladimirovna.* (Composed 2003. Original work published 2014 in Russian, ISBN 9781310150340.). San Diego, CA: HPA Press. ISBN 9781311970152

Davydov, A., & Skorbatyuk, O. (2014). K. Bazilevsky (Trans.). *Ideology Of Religions. Scientific Proof Of Existence Of "God": The Catalog Of Human Population.* (Original work published 2014 in Russian, ISBN 9781311946690.). San Diego, CA: HPA Press. ISBN 9781311413932 ISBN 9780988648593

Political Science

Davydov, A. (2014). K. Bazilevsky (Trans.). *Essence Of Political Ideologies And Their Role In The Historical Process (Political History Of Russia).* (Composed 2003. Original work published 2014 in Russian, ISBN 9781310199929.). San Diego, CA: HPA Press. ISBN 9781310199929

Davydov, A. (2014). K. Bazilevsky (Trans.). *Influence Of Psychophysiological Specifics Of A Leader On The Style Of Political Decision-Making.* (Composed 2003. Original work published 2014 in Russian, ISBN 9781310037832). San Diego, CA: HPA Press. ISBN 9781310104558

Davydov, A. (2014). K. Bazilevsky (Trans.). *Elitist Political Concepts.* (Composed 2005. Original work published 2014 in Russian, ISBN 9781310223228). San Diego, CA: HPA Press. ISBN 9781310822858

General Non-Fiction

Bazilevsky, K. (2012). *Human Population Academy: Laws of Human Nature Based on Shan Hai Jing Research Discoveries by A. Davydov & O. Skorbatyuk.* San Diego, CA: HPA Press. ISBN 9781301986781 ISBN 9780988648500

Davydov, A. (2013). *Shan Khay Tszin: Mify Ili Struktura Psikhiki?* [Shan Hai Jing: Myths Or Structure Of Psyche?] (Composed 1999. Originally pub. 1999 in Russian in Moscow: *Power Of Spirit*, 32-35.). Marina Del Rey, CA: Catalog Of Human Souls GP. ISBN 9781301590391

Davydov, A. (2013). *"Shan Khay Tszin" i "I Tszin" – Karta Psikhofiziologicheskoy Struktury Cheloveka?* [Shan Hai Jing and I Ching – Map of Human Psychophysiological Structure?] (Composed 2002.). Marina Del Rey, CA: Catalog Of Human Souls GP. ISBN 9781301510009

Davydov, A., & Skorbatyuk, O. (2014). K. Bazilevsky (Trans.). *AHNENERBE: Your Killer Is Under Your Skin* (Original work published 2014 in Russian, ISBN 9781311356741.). San Diego, CA: HPA Press. ISBN 9781311266682

A Man And A Woman – Non-Fiction Series

A Log With Legs Spread Wide

Davydov, A., & Skorbatyuk, O. (2014). K. Bazilevsky (Trans.). *A Log With Legs Spread Wide: Vol. 1. How Men Turn Women Into Nothing.* (Original work published 2014 in Russian, ISBN 9781310388125.). San Diego, CA: HPA Press. ISBN 9781311155771

Davydov, A., & Skorbatyuk, O. (2014). K. Bazilevsky (Trans.). *A Log With Legs Spread Wide: Vol. 2. How Goddesses Are Turned Into Logs. World History Of Turning Women Into Mats.* (Original work published 2014 in Russian, ISBN 9781311238894.). San Diego, CA: HPA Press. ISBN 9781311915603

Davydov, A., & Skorbatyuk, O. (2013). *A Log With Legs Spread Wide: Vol. 3. Women's Thirst For Power Over Men Is The Pathway To Become A*

Garbage. (Original work published 2013 in Russian, ISBN 9781301553075.). Marina Del Rey, CA: Catalog Of Human Souls GP. ISBN 9781301435500

Davydov, A., & Skorbatyuk, O. (2013). *A Log With Legs Spread Wide: Vol. 4. The Head – In The Underpants.* (Original work published 2013 in Russian, ISBN 9781301051281.). Marina Del Rey, CA: Catalog Of Human Souls GP.

Manipulative Games For Women

Davydov, A., & Skorbatyuk, O. (2013). *Manipulyativnyye Igry Dlya Zhenshchin* [Manipulative Games For Women]: *Vol. 1. March 23: Instruction for Exploitation of Men* (2nd ed., in Russian. Original work published 2005, Moscow: SNIALTotems. ISBN 9785716101333). Marina Del Rey, CA: Catalog Of Human Souls GP. ISBN 9781301803521

Davydov, A., & Skorbatyuk, O. (2013). *Manipulyativnyye Igry Dlya Zhenshchin* [Manipulative Games For Women]: *Vol. 2. April 6: Instruction for Exploitation of Men* (2nd ed., in Russian. Original work published 2005, Moscow: SNIALTotems. ISBN 9785716101302). Marina Del Rey, CA: Catalog Of Human Souls GP. ISBN 9781301069286

Davydov, A., & Skorbatyuk, O. (2013). *Manipulyativnyye Igry Dlya Zhenshchin* [Manipulative Games For Women]: *Vol. 3. October 13: Instruction for Exploitation of Men* (2nd ed., in Russian. Original work published 2005, Moscow: SNIALTotems. ISBN 9785716101326). Marina Del Rey, CA: Catalog Of Human Souls GP. ISBN 9781301900824

Davydov, A., & Skorbatyuk, O. (2013). *Manipulyativnyye Igry Dlya Zhenshchin* [Manipulative Games For Women]: *Vol. 4. December 7: Instruction for Exploitation of Men* (2nd ed., in Russian. Original work published 2005, Moscow: SNIALTotems. ISBN 9785716101319). Marina Del Rey, CA: Catalog Of Human Souls GP. ISBN 9781301413065

Secret Sexual Desires

Bazilevsky, K. (2013). *How To Seduce Men/Women Born On <Date> Or Secret Sexual Desires of 10 Million People: Demo From Shan Hai Jing Research Discoveries by A. Davydov & O. Skorbatyuk.* (Vols. 1-10). San Diego, CA: HPA Press.

Bazilevsky, K. (2013). *How To Seduce Men & Women Born On March 5 Or Secret Sexual Desires of 20 Million People: Demo From Shan Hai Jing Research Discoveries by A. Davydov & O. Skorbatyuk.* San Diego, CA: HPA Press. ISBN 9781301087204

Bazilevsky, K. (2013). *Secret Sexual Desires of 100 Million People—Seduction Recipes For Men & Women: Demos From Shan Hai Jing Research Discoveries by A. Davydov & O. Skorbatyuk.* San Diego, CA: HPA Press. ISBN 9780988648579 ISBN 9781301135035 ISBN 9780988648586

A list of other publications related to our scientific research can be found at http://www.humanpopulationacademy.org/publications/.

CONNECT WITH US

1. Visit our official website.

Human Population Academy and Special Scientific Info-Analytical Laboratory—Catalog of Human Souls:
https://www.HumanPopulationAcademy.org

2. Connect with us on social networks.

- ❖ *Facebook* - http://www.facebook.com/HumanPopulationAcademy (Note: you must be logged in to *Facebook* in order to access this page.)
- ❖ *YouTube* - http://www.youtube.com/user/HumanPopulAcademy
- ❖ *Google+* - http://plus.google.com/+HumanpopulationacademyOrghumannature
- ❖ *LinkedIn* - http://www.linkedin.com/company/2484433
- ❖ *Pinterest* - http://pinterest.com/humanpopacademy/
- ❖ *Twitter* - http://twitter.com/HumanPopAcademy

3. Contact us.

You can find out how to contact us at the Human Population Academy's website under Contacts (see https://www.humanpopulationacademy.org/breakthrough-discovery/contacts/).

ABOUT US

Special Scientific Info-Analytical Laboratory—Catalog of Human Souls was founded by Andrey Davydov. The laboratory is engaged in research and decryption of the ancient Chinese monument Shan Hai Jing, as well as other ancient texts, and creation of the *Catalog of Human Population*. The technology of uncovering individual structures of psyche of *Homo sapiens* for this Catalog was developed by Andrey Davydov; it is not based on any existing domestic or foreign research, methods or theoretical concepts. The laboratory is a partner with the Human Population Academy.

Human Population Academy was founded by Kate Bazilevsky. The Academy's mission is to inform all of over 7 billion humans living on Earth about the discovery of the *Catalog of Human Population*. The Academy educates about the *Catalog of Human Population* (*Catalog of Human Souls*) and provides access to informational materials from this Catalog to the public.

LEADERSHIP

ANDREY DAVYDOV

Research Supervisor of the Special Scientific Info-Analytical Laboratory—Catalog of Human Souls

Andrey Davydov is an expert in Chinese culture, researcher of ancient texts, the author of scientific discovery of the *Catalog of Human Population* and the technology of decryption of the ancient Chinese monument Shan Hai

Jing as the *Catalog of Human Population*. He authored over 300 published books, including scientific monographs and ideologies. In 2012, he was granted political asylum in the USA due to persecution by a group of employees of the Federal Security Service of Russian Federation (FSB, formerly KGB), who decided to expropriate his research product—the *Catalog of Human Population*.

OLGA SKORBATYUK

Senior Analyst at the Special Scientific Info-Analytical Laboratory—Catalog of Human Souls

Olga Skorbatyuk is a professional psychologist, one of the developers of the *Catalog of Human Population*, the founder of Non-Traditional Psychoanalysis, and co-author of over 300 books and scientific articles. She was granted political asylum in the USA together with A. Davydov.

KATE BAZILEVSKY

Founder of the Human Population Academy, Junior Analyst at the Special Scientific Info-Analytical Laboratory—Catalog of Human Souls

Kate Bazilevsky is the director of the Human Population Academy, a Junior Analyst at the Catalog of Human Souls laboratory, an author and a translator of books about the *Catalog of Human Population*. She holds a degree in MIS and psychology. She founded the Human Population Academy in 2011 and a publishing company called HPA Press in 2012.

www.ingramcontent.com/pod-product-compliance
Lightning Source LLC
Chambersburg PA
CBHW072134020426
42334CB00018B/1794